HEAVEN

Can't Wait

A Survey of Alleged Trips to the Other Side

William M. Alnor

Foreword by Tal Brooke

Baker Books
A Division of Baker Book House Co
Grand Rapids, Michigan 49516

Published by Baker Books
a division of Baker Book House Company
P.O. Box 6287, Grand Rapids, MI 49516-6287

Printed in the United States of America

Library of Congress Cataloging-in-Publication Data

Alnor, William M.
    Heaven can't wait : a survey of alleged trips to the other side /
William M. Alnor.
      p.   cm.
    Includes bibliographical references and indexes.
    ISBN 0-8010-5284-X (pbk.)
    1. Death—Religious aspects—Christianity. 2. Future life—Christianity. 3. Near-death experiences—Religious aspects—Controversial literature. 4. Near-death experiences—Religious aspects—Christianity. 5. Occultism—Controversial literature. 6. Occultism—Religious aspects—Christianity. 7. Spiritualism—Controversial literature. 8. Prophecies—Christianity—Controversial literature. 9. Visions—Controversial literature. I. Title.
BT825.A38   1995
133.9'01'—dc20   95-32778

To my parents,
Warren and Jean Alnor,
who have helped to guide me all these years

Contents

Foreword

America is being hit with its second wave of public fascination over what happens after death. The first wave of interest hit in the 1970s when publicized reports of "near-death experiences" first appeared. More recently two accounts about near-death experiences, those of Betty Eadie and Dannion Brinkley, have remained at the top of the best-seller list. What is different about this second wave is that the public seems ready to accept these reports at face value. And this includes a large cross section of Christians who have broken rank, crossing over into the realm of the occult, without even knowing it.

What takes place after death is a mystery that has occupied the center stage of human interest down the centuries. It is a subject that is timeless. Hearers are always vulnerable to tales about "the other side," a subject perennially close to the human heart. For that reason, new "breakthroughs" are always of interest.

Top cult researcher and journalist Bill Alnor has stepped in at a crucial time with this probing and timely book. And he has done a masterful job. Alnor uses his years of relentless reporting and researching skills as a professional journalist (and journalism professor at Philadelphia's Temple University) to pursue reports and accounts, probing for inconsistencies, changing stories, and outright falsehoods. He combines this relentless journalistic pursuit with sound theological training—his other profession. Bill Alnor exposes things that most people would never find on their own. Alnor also shows Christians who have broken rank exactly where they have wandered—into alien terrain and way out of their depths.

Let's take a look at the issue for a moment. The two waves of public interest are based on the claim that the mystery of death has been "solved" due to new scientific breakthroughs in the realm of advanced resuscitation methods in medical technology. First of all, "death" is diagnosed by a machine and is pronounced when the subject's brain waves appear flat on an EEG machine (an electroencephalograph) while other signs of metabolic stasis are present. The person is "dead" because the machine announces the state of death in the same way that a spark-plug analyzer tells a mechanic that a car has a bad plug. It's right there on the graph. At that point modern medical teams can quickly begin resuscitation using a variety of options.

Those crossing the "deathplane" constitute a growing army of "flatliners" who have presented the world with a growing body of evidence that challenges the deepest and most sacrosanct biblical beliefs. And it all started when their EEGs went flat.

When the clinically dead supposedly return, they come back with a wide range of reports about the afterlife. A number of now-famous researchers, such as Dr. Raymond

Moody and Dr. Elisabeth Kübler-Ross, have testified to the reality of these near-death experiences, while at the same time going a step further. They interpret the ultimate meaning of these reports, and here is where science bridges over to religion.

The more famous death experiences of Betty Eadie and Dannion Brinkley embody all of the attributes of deathplane encounters outlined in the super best-seller and pioneering work on the subject, Raymond Moody's *Life after Life;* they go further and deeper than the rest. The memory of the event is more intact, while the person undergoes remarkable changes, often becoming psychic. Most stay in contact with their spirit guide, guardian angel, or being of light, while receiving guidance from dreams and revelations. They are connected to the other side in a special way. And this becomes apparent whenever they are interviewed in the mass media.

Tabulating these variant death experiences has opened up a Pandora's box that plays perfectly into the hands of those—many at the helm of New Age leadership—who seek to unify the biblical view with the occult tradition. For naive Christians this is a deadly endeavor. If you accept the game by its own rules, it is an inescapable trap. Moody, by opening up argument-by-experience, then tabulating the pattern of experiences, has created this trap. The argument in essence amounts to this: *If you believe in one report you are forced to believe them all,* and then you are left to tabulate them through a sort of voting system with majority rule. It works in your favor if you are a pantheist/New Ager or Universalist. The net of belief can only get wider; it cannot get narrower. What happens to "the narrow way"? It becomes wider, much wider.

In these near-death reports we see a strange alliance that has come into play between two unlikely allies—

science and the supernatural. But it is a graft that won't fully work because science, by definition, can only work in the objective—not subjective—realm and it can only do so by using outwardly observable quantifiable data. What happens in the subjective interior is out of bounds. This "scientific supernaturalism" of the near-death experience does seem to pull heaven out of the magician's hat. And this is a powerful drawing card. In this heaven, the historical transcendent Christ is just one more being of light in an endless pantheon of luminous cosmic beings.

In the scientific supernatural near-death experience, we also see the makings of a spiritual module waiting to be plugged into any world religion. It seems to span world religions by using the afterlife as its bridge. Thus it is the new inclusive faith that judges no one and admits all—universalism. It is the sort of great deception that the pages of the Bible have warned about for almost two thousand years. That is the nature of deception—something looks good but is lethal.

Bill Alnor shows us how the real effect of the near-death paradigm, originally presented by Dr. Raymond Moody, is to deliver the fun-loving public from the hard truths of orthodox Christianity. It offers people an escape from the consequences of their actions by portraying a lenient and permissive deathplane and afterlife. The near-death revelations from which this view comes have become sweet lies that look harmless and inviting—like the fruit in the garden—and because of that allure, they are even more devastating. Bill Alnor's work is a timely antidote to this fast-moving spiritual virus.

Tal Brooke
President, Spiritual Counterfeits Project

Tal Brooke, President & Chairman of SCP, Inc., is author of the best-seller, *When the World Will Be as One,* and *Lord of the Air*—which chronicles his years in India as the top Western disciple of the famed godman of "Signs & Wonders," Sai Baba—plus four other books. He has degrees from the University of Virginia [Col.] and Princeton [Theol.], and has spoken at Oxford and Cambridge numerous times among other prominent universities.

Acknowledgments

This book would not have been done without the help a number of people gave me. The Spiritual Counterfeits Project president, Tal Brooke, shared some of his insights with me on the topic during a ride back from a conference in Maryland. Later some of his writings stimulated some of my thinking in the area of near-death experiences as it appears that the East, in the form of mysticism and occultism, has once again invaded the West. Thanks also goes to the *Christian Research Journal*. Its editor asked me to write an article on this topic several years ago, which was a significant push behind this book. Audio and video expert Rolly DeVore also chipped in by sending me a videotape that related to the topic. Later, during the course of my writing, Dr. Ron Rhodes, one of America's foremost apologists, answered some late-breaking questions on angels. But my main helper/researcher in this project was, as always, my wife Jackie. She helped supply me with documentation (and transcripts) of the shenanigans going on in the world of televangelism that directly relate to the upcoming pages. My main prayer for this book is that it can help the church in these last days sort through the deception of the maze of mysticism. Thanks to everyone!

Introduction

The scene was a book convention in the San Francisco area. That afternoon more than one hundred people were waiting in a curved line that snaked all the way to the back of the spacious room.

They were waiting for their chance to speak with best-selling author Betty Eadie, and perhaps to get her autograph. Many of them had tears in their eyes when they finally reached her.

"My mom gave me this book Christmas Day," sobbed a blond-haired woman to Eadie, "the day before she died in a car accident and your book really made me feel better about where she is now."[1]

In her first book, *Embraced by the Light,* Betty Eadie says she knows where everyone goes after death—to heaven, of course. And her book, promising hope to all, struck a nerve on planet earth. More than two million copies of *Embraced by the Light* have been published in twenty-one languages, and the book has been on the *New York Times* best-seller list for over a year.

At another speaking engagement Eadie, who claims to have had a near-death experience more than nineteen years ago during which she was literally embraced by Jesus in heaven, tells a rapt audience about the spirituality she gleaned from the other side. "I learned that we are all divine by nature," she says. "Each and every one of us is divine. Perfect. When we come down to earth we become mutated."[2]

Later she told *20/20*'s Hugh Downs that she believes that all the negative things in life are necessary in order for us to have the positive. Her message is very comfortable to the masses—everyone makes it in the end.

Near-death experiences, or NDEs, have been told and retold since almost the dawn of history, even though they weren't always known as NDEs. But today, perhaps because of better communication and advances in medicine that enable medical personnel to prolong life during dire medical emergencies—and even to bring people back from the brink of death after their bodily functions cease—we know a lot more about the topic.

Part of the reason is the pioneering work by Dr. Raymond Moody, a medical doctor, who in 1975 published *Life after Life* which chronicled accounts of many people who claim they've died or have been near death, and have gone through similar experiences of entering a tunnel and sometimes viewing a bright light along with a fleeting look at the next world. *Life after Life* became a runaway best-seller and it continues to sell briskly. By 1990 more than three million copies were in circulation after forty-two printings.

In explaining his groundbreaking book, Moody wrote in the introduction that he didn't come into his study of the afterlife with many theological presuppositions; he was tolerant and respectful of all faiths. "I believe that all the great religions of man have many truths to tell us," he writes, "and I believe that no one of us has all the answers to the deep and fundamental truths with which religion deals. In organizational terms, I am a member of the Methodist Church."[3]

However, many of the NDEs recounted in his book are of a religious nature. Numerous people have testified to seeing Jesus. It's troubling to some readers that the portrait of Jesus described by Moody's patients seems to be at variance with the Jesus of the biblical record. Moody's "Jesus" was a savior who did not die for the sins of the world. He was an avatar in the next world that was more concerned about what people were learning or cosmic evolution than with sin. And Moody documented accounts from some patients of non-Christian religious leaders such as Mohammed and Buddha greeting people on the other side. Indeed, there were shades of Eadie's basic comfortable message of universalism in *Life after Life*—that everyone makes it in the end.

What a switch from the hell and damnation preachers of yesterday! Certainly Jonathan Edwards's pre-Revolutionary War sermon "Sinners in the Hands of an Angry God" would not be spiritually attractive to the masses enthralled by these stories.

Today, nearly twenty years after publication of *Life after Life*, Moody lives in Alabama, and his theology has apparently been replaced with the spirituality of New Age occultism—a repackaged form of Hinduism mixed with things like astrology, tarot cards, ESP, channeling (spiritism), UFOs, and many other practices. Moody is a frequent lecturer at New Age conferences, and his new perspective has more in common with the religion of Shirley MacLaine than with John Wesley's Methodism.

Moody is now deeply involved in spiritism—he has devoted a large part of his time researching methods to communicate with the spirits of the dead, concentrating on his own ancestors—an act specifically condemned in both the Old and New Testaments.[4]

On a recent national television show that explored the ongoing obsession with NDEs, ABC's Diane Sawyer interviewed Moody at his home. Moody claimed that he has not only succeeded in contacting the dead, but has had intense encounters and dialogues with their spirits. He took Sawyer to his attic, an isolated room covered with mirrors on the ceiling and walls with a meditation chair in the center, and left her sitting there for more than a half hour in the chair. (Sawyer, following Moody's instructions, experimented to see whether Moody's room actually was a doorway to the spirit realm. She emerged from the attic with a smirk on her face, claiming that it didn't work for her.)

Since Moody's groundbreaking book, he has written others such as *Reflections on Life after Life, The Light Beyond,* and his latest work, *Reunions: Visionary Encounters with Departed Loved Ones.*

During this same time period in the Christian world, stories of NDEs and the afterlife spilled over into the marketplace. Pat Robertson's *700 Club* television show has featured many stories over the years from people who claim to have briefly died and returned. And on the Trinity Broadcasting Network, the world's largest Christian network, popular repeat guest Dr. Richard Eby also claims to have had several glimpses of the other side (including a glimpse of hell). Other Christian writers such as Betty Malz, author of six books that deal (in varying degrees) with her own near-death experience, have been making the rounds on Christian radio and television, and doing seminars in churches and retreats. One of Malz's books, *My Glimpse of Eternity,* has sold around one million copies and has been printed in eleven languages.

And increasingly, on the charismatic/Pentecostal side of the church, which has always been more experience-driven than the evangelical or fundamentalist side, a trend of stories about alleged trips to heaven and hell are on the rise with a growing number of evangelists, some of whom have achieved international notoriety.

The current "holy laughter" movement that has taken the world by storm is yet another piece of the puzzle. Although there are many people involved in holy laughter, most agree that Rodney Howard-Browne, an evangelist from South Africa, is the main force behind popularizing it. Taking various verses of Scripture out of context, Howard-Browne invites people to get "drunk" on the Holy Spirit, and during his talk laughter breaks out throughout the auditorium. His influence has landed him as a repeat guest on Paul and Jan Crouch's Trinity Broadcasting Network (TBN), and in recent days Howard-Browne has been credited with affecting the John Wimber–affiliated Vineyard churches with this phenomenon, spurring an outbreak of holy laughter and other mystical marvels known as the Toronto Blessing.

During a summer 1994 TBN appearance Howard-Browne told the Crouches that one woman who was overcome with the "new wine" of the holy laughter experience was suddenly transported to heaven where she saw Jesus "leaning against a rock." There she saw her daughter whom she had aborted twenty years earlier, smiling and saying, "Look at Mommy, Jesus. She's laughing."

"Another woman that had aborted twins, same similar type thing," Howard-Browne continued on the show. "She found the power of God and was out for probably over an hour. The next thing she was in heaven. You know, a vision. God just took her right in, and two children come running to her and flung their arms around her and said, 'Mommy, we forgive you.' Well, you know that might not mean a lot to other people but to these people that are carrying hurts and things, God is setting them free."[5]

What are we to make of all these stories? Have people really traveled to heaven to meet Jesus? Have they really had glimpses of the other side? Or have they simply had visions of the other side? And are these visions divine or wishful thinking? There are other questions with worse implications. Are the writers and preachers of these tales fakers, weaving these far-out stories for financial benefit? Have they been influenced by the occult? Or are there other factors, such as medical considerations, that are responsible for some of these experiences?

Why is it for so many people that heaven can't wait? These are questions I pondered during the past several years researching this book.

In looking into these questions I have discovered that in some cases there may be legitimate medical explanations that may be able to account for some NDEs.

But they can't explain all of them away, and most of these are unproven—after all, everything is unproven when we deal with the afterlife and the heavenly realm of God—for God's ways are higher than our ways.

What *can* be proven, though, is that most accounts of heaven dramatically contradict each other in significant ways, conclusively showing that if these people's souls actually went to a real place, they didn't go to the same place they thought was heaven. One doesn't have to go any further than to look at the two accounts of heaven presented to us by the two secular best-sellers of 1994 that deal with NDEs: Eadie's *Embraced by the Light,* and Dannion Brinkley's *Saved by the Light.* In Eadie's tale, Jesus allegedly plays a major role in heaven. He greets her there and divulges many mysteries to her. In Brinkley's account Jesus is absent from heaven. Heaven seems to be run by a council of thirteen elders, twelve of whom correspond to the signs of the zodiac! Contradictions like these, despite some similarities, are enormous.

Second, accounts of heaven from visionaries throughout the centuries have been contradictory. These views of the next life through ancient NDEs, dreams, visions, and alleged revelations in past times seem to reflect the prevailing ideas of the afterlife presented during their respective ages. That may be how we have received, for example, the popular medieval images of angels in heaven having halos and of heavenly dwellers sitting on clouds. We'll look at this in more depth later.

Third, it has become obvious to the discerning Christian that the entire field of NDE research and even elements of the "I went to heaven" craze circulating through the Christian church has become an area of massive spiritual deception, an assault against the historic Christian faith, and an attack against the person, nature, and work of Jesus Christ.

Fourth, in the charismatic and Pentecostal movements, as we shall see, these alleged trips to heaven seem to fulfill the dual purposes of creating spiritual elitism—to establish a speaker's credentials in the eyes of a gullible public—and using these fantastic stories to scratch their followers' itching ears. In short, these stories are the type people want to hear—even if they can't be documented or proven.

Finally, and most important, one of the unfortunate things about many of the most popular "I went to heaven" stories circulating through the church today is that they contradict God's Word, the Bible, often in significant ways.

All of these stories, both secular and Christian, may have something to tell us about ourselves and contemporary microwavable culture that is uncomfortable with the "old time" Scripture-based religion of Jonathan Edwards and John Wesley. Spiritual Counterfeits Project president Tal Brooke, a friend of Dr. Raymond Moody years ago at the University of Virginia, correctly notes that:

> Indeed, almost every book today on the subject of the afterlife tries to unify the biblical and occult tradition and say that they both reveal the same truth and that both point to the same god. Other books are more blatantly New Age and simply establish that as the reigning worldview.[6]

Brooke also has some words of wisdom concerning the proper use of experience in the life of believers:

> Scripture is, and must be by its own definition, the supreme test of reality and the measure by which mortals are to weigh and discern all things, *including experience.*
> Experience can appear to be one thing and yet be another. Experiences can lie. Indeed, experience is almost always at the doorway of deception, from LSD visions and simple magician's tricks, all the way to the world-class illusions of David Copperfield, Shamanistic and yogic trances, or hypnotic mind-control techniques. It is common knowledge that mental institu-

tions are filled with people who are constantly experiencing things as reality that are not real at all. A private experience of something does not qualify it as ultimate truth.

The deceptive nature of these recent near death experiences is that they seem to finally and fully replace the biblical portrayal of what happens at death. And to replace is to destroy.[7]

Paul warns in 2 Timothy 4, that "the time will come when men will not put up with sound doctrine. Instead, to suit their own desires, they will gather around them a great number of teachers to say what their itching ears want to hear. They will turn their ears away from the truth and turn aside to myths" (vv. 3–4).

1

A Magical Mystery Tour

Consider the following snapshots from the world of contemporary Christianity:

- Charismatic leader Roberts Liardon says he had an extraordinary experience. One afternoon in 1974 when he was eight years old he was caught up into heaven where he met Jesus face-to-face. Liardon of Laguna Hills, California, described Jesus Christ in his book *I Saw Heaven* as "about six feet tall, with sandy-brown hair, not real short and not too long." Jesus escorted him through the gates of heaven where he saw golden streets, dazzling looking flowers, plenty of mansions, trees that "swayed back and forth, dancing and praising as we passed," and a "knee-deep . . . crystal clear" River of Life.¹

On walking to the river, "do you know the first thing Jesus did to me?" Liardon asks. "He dunked me! I got back up and splashed Him, and we had a water fight. We splashed each other and laughed."²

- Prominent inner healing teacher John Sandford of Elijah House ministries declared himself to be a prophet in his January 1991 newsletter. And in his new role he has exciting ideas—like wrestling with demons.

"Last night I wrestled against demonic beings from 3:00 A.M. until just before dawn," he boasted in the newsletter. "And the names the Lord gave me were Samyasa and particularly Azaziel! Have they already been released? Or did I only wrestle with apparitions such as appeared 800 years ago?"³

It wasn't the first time Sandford claims to have been in a wrestling match with beings from the other side. In his book, *Transformation of the Inner Man,* which has gone on to become popular in some Christian circles, he wrote that he wrestled with a dead woman—Agnes Sanford, the pantheistic originator of the inner healing movement.

"Agnes came through my front door (without bothering to open it) and tackled me. We wrestled all over my living room floor (Gen. 32:24–32). . . . She then went out the door beckoning me to follow, and went through the night to a tall tower . . . from floor to floor turning on lights. Ever since then the Lord has been turning on lights in my 'tower of knowledge.'"⁴

- Benny Hinn, the best-selling author and pastor of the Orlando Christian Center bragged on the Trinity Broadcasting Network's February 11, 1992, *Praise the Lord* program that he frequently wakes up in the middle of the night to "literally see forms of angels" appear in his bedroom in different shapes. One night he saw a man in his bedroom who was "wrapped in fire," he said. Then a blond-haired entity came into his room and whisked him away by the hand, showing him a multitude of people being shoved into a valley of "liquid fire," he told TBN founders Paul and Jan Crouch, who were amazed by Hinn's vision.

- Evangelist Oral Roberts claims that the devil himself walked into his bedroom in February 1987 and almost choked him to death.

  "I felt those hands on my throat and he was choking the life out of me," Roberts said in an appearance on his son's television program, *Richard Roberts Live*. "I yelled to my wife, 'Honey, come!'" Evelyn Roberts responded by rushing to his room, laid hands on him and "rebuked the devil and commanded the devil to get out of his room," Roberts declared. "I began to breathe and came out of my bed strong."[5]

But as we might guess, many of the claims made in the name of experience—even Christian claims—today are not biblical or even truthful.

Take the just-mentioned Oral Roberts story about the devil in his room. It was one of the outlandish stories Roberts spun in 1987 during the media hubbub over his "give me eight million dollars or I die" fundraising appeals. But considering Roberts's history, the fundraising scheme or his fight with the devil was not unusual. More than a decade before, Roberts announced that he spoke to a nine-hundred-foot-tall image of Jesus,[6] who commanded him to build a sixty-story City of Faith Hospital in Tulsa, Oklahoma, where Jesus said a cure for cancer would be found!

Today, however, it is obvious that God had not spoken. The financially strapped Roberts empire was forced to quietly sell off the complex several years ago—without finding a cure for cancer.

Visions of the Demonic

In the circles Roberts has thrived in—a camp within the Christian church often associated with the Pentecostal and charismatic movements—alleged visions of the spirit realm and glimpses of the supernatural are popular, with all sorts of teachers parlaying these and other subjective experiences into messages eagerly devoured by their followers.

These include many alleged trips to heaven (and sometimes hell) by charismatic and Pentecostal leaders (including those in the Word-Faith camp). Their stories are told in first-person accounts on Christian radio and television, on audio and video teaching tapes, and especially in books and newsletters. Perhaps not so coincidentally this Christian fascination with alleged heavenly visits seems to be increasing at the same pace as the public's fascination with glimpses of the other side via near-death experiences (NDEs).

Some of these written accounts have gone on to become Christian best-sellers, mirroring the secular successes of Betty Eadie's *Embraced by the Light* and Dannion Brinkley's *Saved by the Light*. It is finally at the point where many internationally known charismatic leaders have claimed to have been to heaven and back—and most of these alleged experiences were not NDEs.

Some of this is no doubt opportunism at its worst. Disgraced television evangelist/faith healer Peter Popoff, who was exposed on the *Tonight Show* with Johnny Carson in May 1986 for having a miniature radio receiver in his ear while his wife was transmitting details to him about audience members' ailments, has been back on TV in recent years. His repertoire includes his new book *7 Hours in Heaven!* in which he boasts that he was whisked up to heaven and was shown his future lavish mansion and was personally commissioned by Jesus Christ to prepare the earth for a new outpouring of the Holy Spirit.[7] Popoff, speaking at a crusade in Philadelphia, claims to have the ability to dispatch angels at his whim for a gift of forty dollars.

Near-Death Experiences and Visits to Heaven

Although this book discusses what has come to be known as near-death experiences, a large portion of it will deal with the increasing mystical fascination with the next world circulating through the church today. These otherworldly stories are related to NDEs, but *they aren't the same thing.*

These "I went to heaven and hell" experiences are different than NDEs because those who claim to have experienced them are not necessarily near death when they happened. They are usually more mystical and are often more detailed than the typical NDE. Sometimes those who claim to have been to the other side were not sure if they were actually there or if they were shown a vision.

Second, Christians are reporting these experiences. They seem to be closely related to an emphasis on signs and wonders that is sweeping through the charismatic and Pentecostal movements.

NDEs became popular following the publication of Moody's book in 1975. In a typical NDE, a hospital patient who is near death (or who has temporarily stopped breathing or who has experienced a severe heart attack or trauma that has caused the heart to stop beating) often testifies to finding himself hovering above his body, then being propelled through a dark tunnel toward a bright light on the other side. Moody identifies up to fifteen stages related to NDEs that people can go through.

NDEs are not necessarily Christian-based; NDEs don't necessarily reflect a worldview that includes the godhead (represented by the Holy Trinity) on one side and the devil and his hoards on the other, as is often the case in these "I went to heaven (and sometimes hell)" stories.

In recent years I have examined many of the most popular "I went to heaven" stories circulating through the church. As a result of my inquiry I am throwing up a bright red flag of caution over believing *any* of the current heaven or hell visitation stories. We cannot trust them. The stories are confusing at times partly due to their mystical nature. But they are usually contradictory on significant details. Out of all the stories I've examined there were no perfect matches. In other words one man's picture of heaven did not correlate with the pictures given to us by any of the others.

Other serious objections include: Their portraits of heaven and hell do not seem to correlate with the biblical record on these two domains; the stories are unverifiable and mystical—there's no way to put any of them to the test—and many of the stories seem to serve the purpose of establishing the storyteller's ministry or credentials as being especially anointed or favored by Christ over others. In many cases they use these tales to validate claims that they have apostolic-type ministries.

For example Roberts Liardon claims that during his childhood visit, he was ordained! "Roberts, I am calling you to a great work," Jesus allegedly told him. "I am ordaining you to a great work. You will have to run like no one else and preach like no one else. You will have to be different from everyone else."[8]

Most serious of all, perhaps, is that many of the stories are unbiblical in the sense that they are used to promote false doctrine. Take Roberts Liardon's fanciful tale, for example. Liardon claims that after his water fight with Christ, Jesus walked him to the heavenly throne room of God where he noticed "three storage houses 500 to 600 yards" away. He explains:

> We walked into the first. As Jesus shut the front door behind us, I looked around the interior in shock! On one side of the building were exterior parts of the body. Legs hung from the wall, but the scene looked natural, not grotesque. On the other side of the building were shelves filled with eyes, green ones, brown ones, blue ones, and so forth.
>
> The building contained all of the parts of the human body that people on earth need, but Christians have not realized these blessings are waiting in heaven. There is no place else in the universe for these parts to go except right here on earth; no one else needs them.
>
> Jesus said to me, "These are the unclaimed blessings. This building should not be full. It should be emptied. You should come in here with faith and get the needed parts for you, and the people you will come in contact with that day."
>
> The unclaimed blessings are there in those storehouses—all of the parts of the body people might need: hundreds of new eyes, legs, skin, hair, eardrums—they

are all there. All you have to do is go in and get what you need by the arm of faith, because it is there.[9]

In making these claims Liardon is subtly using his special heavenly revelations to promote the "name it and claim it" false prosperity doctrines that have ravaged the Christian church like a cancer in these last days.

You do not have to cry and beg God to make the part you need. Just go get it. The doors to the storehouses are never locked. They are always open for those who need to go in. We should empty those buildings.

. . . Because of my visit to heaven, I never had any doubt that Jesus not only wants His people well and whole but that healing is available for any who will receive. I knew beyond the shadow of a doubt that God did not put sickness and disease on people. I saw no sickness and disease in heaven during my visit, only provision for creative miracles.[10]

A Word of Caution

Of course it is possible for God's children to be caught up into heaven. God is God. He has the prerogative of doing whatever he wishes. But we need to be wary of leaders who claim an exclusive vision or experience in order to verify their ministries. Christian leaders should point others to Christ and what he has done on the cross instead of to their own personal experiences. Most of these people claiming heavenly visitations seem to have a much different attitude about their alleged experiences than the apostle Paul had when he discussed his trip (whether in the spirit or body) to the "third heaven" in 2 Corinthians 12. In the verses leading up to his account of heaven, Paul was clearly reluctant to discuss his experiences because he thought he would be perceived as "boasting" about it.[11]

On the contrary, many of today's "travelers" to heaven revel in their alleged experiences, and discuss them before packed halls without reluctance. Christian media outlets such as Pat Robertson's *700 Club* and TBN often give extensive airtime to these tales. And these experiences, at least in a few of the cases, seem to form the central planks of their ministries. In the typical story circulating through the church today one is taken to heaven to consult with Jesus or deceased saints. Besides witnessing incredible sights, most of them claim they were commissioned there or specially anointed for their ministries in heaven, often by Jesus himself.

John MacArthur warns that we need to be wary of any of these stories if their agenda appears to be to promote a "special anointing" of a leader.

> Mysticism is still very much alive, still using spiritual intimidation to demean the uninitiated. People today who claim to have had heavenly visions or spellbinding experiences are often simply puffed up with idle notions, using their claims to intimidate others into elevating them. As the apostle Paul wrote the Colossian believers, that kind of mysticism is the product of a prideful and unspiritual mind.[12]

Visitors to the Other Side

On the June 30, 1992, *700 Club* telecast, a medical doctor identified as Gerald Landrey testified that after he suffered cardiac arrest he found himself instantly in heaven for the "most glorious experience" he ever had. He said that on the other side people welcomed him in a bright place where people were "loving each other like we never loved before." He then said he witnessed an explosion of light and saw Jesus Christ on the cross. Jesus, whom he described as having "dark hair" and looking "very Jewish" then promised him that he would be healed of his heart condition and back home within a week—which he was.

David Yonggi Cho

Although Landrey has not become a prominent name for his alleged heavenly trip, some of the biggest names in the charismatic movement claim to have visited heaven. David (Paul) Yonggi Cho of Seoul, Korea, controversial pastor of the largest church in the world (with more than five-hundred-thousand members), claims he has been to the other side and back. He said he met a blue-skinned deceased missionary to Korea there who commissioned him to reach his country folk for Christ.[13] Cho has also stated that one of his assistant pastors at the Yoido Full Gospel Church died and came back to life after three days. During that time period, Cho stated in an interview with Mary Stewart Relfe, his assistant pastor was reunited with his wife in heaven where he saw God and was able to meet various biblical figures including Abraham, Stephen, and David.[14]

Kenneth Hagin

Another who claims to have been to heaven and also hell is prominent radio evangelist Kenneth E. Hagin, founder of the RHEMA Bible Training Center in Tulsa, Oklahoma. In his book *I Believe in Visions,* he claims that as a young man in 1933, suffering from a deformed heart and incurable blood disease, his heart stopped beating and his "inner man rushed out of my body . . . [and] . . . I went down, down, down until the lights of the earth faded away. . . . And the farther down I went, the hotter and more stifling it became. Finally, far below me, I could see lights flickering on the walls of the caverns of the damned. . . . I came to the entrance of hell."[15] Hagin stated that a voice from above, Christ's voice, rescued him from hell during the occasion (as well as two other subsequent times when his heart also stopped beating) as he lay deathly ill.

Hagin has also stated that during a revival meeting in Rockwall, Texas, in 1950, Jesus appeared to him, standing in the air near the top of the tent. "Come up hither," Jesus allegedly commanded him in King James English, Hagin wrote. Hagin then claims he sailed through the air with Christ "until we came to a beautiful city. . . . we beheld it at close range as one might go up on a mountain and look down on a city in the valley. Its beauty was beyond words!"[16] He wrote that:

> [Jesus said] people selfishly say they are ready for heaven. They talk about their mansions and the glories of heaven while many around them live in darkness and hopelessness. Jesus said I should share my hope with them and invite them to come to heaven with me.
>
> Then Jesus turned to me and said, "Now let us go down to hell." . . . We came back out of heaven, and when we got to earth we didn't stop, but kept going.
>
> We went down to hell, and as we went into that place I saw what appeared to be human beings wrapped in flames. I said, "Lord, this looks just like it did when I died and came to this place on April 23, 1933. . . . Jesus told me, 'Warn men and women about this place.'"[17]

Hagin also claims that during a trip to heaven, Jesus commissioned him to a special ministry and personally gave him a special anointing to heal the sick.[18]

Morris Cerullo

Well-known Pentecostal evangelist Morris Cerullo, like Hagin, claims to have been caught up into heaven during a service. Cerullo, who has been in the news recently in connection with his failed bid to take over Jim and Tammy Bakker's Heritage USA,[19] says the incident was a "vision" that later evolved into his "spirit lift[ing] from this earth and was taken right into the heavens."[20] There he saw a six-foot-tall "manifestation of the Godhead" that didn't look human at all:

> I am not going to tell you that I saw Jesus with long brown hair, a beautiful beard, and [a] nice long white robe. (I would not discredit anyone who has seen a vision like that, for another's vision could have been just as real as mine.) Directly in front of that great mass of people, the height of an average man, about six feet tall and two feet wide, there appeared a great flaming ball of brightness and glory; it had no physical human features about it at all! There were no eyes, there were no ears, no nose, no mouth, no hands and no legs, but just a great flaming ball of brightness and glory.[21]

He called the entity "the Presence of God, for this light was not just the glory of Jesus but it was the glory of the Godhead; the Father, the Son, and the Holy Ghost." The entity then showed him the fires of hell in which "were multitudes of lost souls."[22] It spoke these words to him in King James English: "My son, arise, shine, for thy light is come and the glory of the Lord is risen upon thee. Thou shalt not be afraid for thou shall not stand in thine own strength, neither shall you stand in thine own place but you shall stand in the place I have made for thee and My strength shall uphold and guard thee."[23]

Jesse Duplantis

Prominent piano-playing evangelist Jesse Duplantis, who has often appeared with Kenneth Copeland at his crusades, claims that while in his hotel room in August 1988 in Magnolia, N.Y., he was "sucked through" the ceiling at a "phenomenal rate of speed" and he found himself in a vehicle that looked like a cross between a ski lift and cable car that was guided by a "blond-headed angel." "You have an appointment with the great God Jehovah," he said the angel told him. The vehicle took him to heaven, which was really another "planet," he said.

While there he saw Peter, James, and John, and met Jonah, Paul, and Abraham; David acted as his tour guide, showing him his lavish super mansion. "*ABC Prime Time* would get mad as a hornet if they saw my house," Duplantis quipped. He also claims he saw animals and plenty of children who were toting harps. He was then taken to Jehovah in the throne room of heaven and to Jesus—who instructed him to go tell people on earth that he's coming back.[24]

Thinking of Things Above

Complicating this discussion is the fact that there's nothing wrong with Christians dwelling on the after-life. God's Word tells us that we are to be oriented toward heaven and the eternal rather than on worldly things. We are to live as "aliens and strangers in the world" (1 Peter 2:11) because "our citizenship is in heaven" (Phil. 3:20). It is healthy, then, for Christians to contemplate our future home in heaven instead of on this planet. Jesus comforted his disciples by assuring them that he was preparing a place for them in heaven (John 14:1–4). But that kind of attention is only healthy when we trust the promises of God, not the visions of someone who asserts things on his own authority. Jeremiah 5:30–31 states: "A horrible and shocking thing has happened in the land: The prophets prophesy lies, the priests rule by their own authority, and my people love it this way. But what will you do in the end?" No legitimate spiritual purpose is served when the afterlife promised to believers in Scripture is described in terms drawn from legend, myth, and superstition.

But there *is* something wrong with these experiences when they contradict what God's revealed Word says about heaven and hell. In Jesse Duplantis's fanciful story he implied the doctrine of the preexistence of souls[25] and he separated the Holy Trinity, even denying the omnipresence of God by claiming that the Holy Spirit is only on earth—and not also in heaven with God the Father and God the Son. He also erred from the truth by claiming that God *needs* love from people, when the fact is that God needs nothing.

The most obvious problem with the "I went to heaven" stories is the clear biblical testimony that heaven is a place beyond our ability to describe. According to Paul, who was "caught up to the third heaven," it was a place where he "heard *inexpressible things, things that man is not permitted to tell*" (2 Cor. 12:2, 4, emphasis mine). Paul, in keeping with Jesus' words about a different type of bodily existence in the future heavenly realm, strongly stated in 1 Corinthians 15:35–54 that the difference between our earthly and heavenly bodies will be great indeed.

With this in mind, the problems inherent with all the "I went to heaven" stories are (1) If Christian leaders today have been caught up to paradise why are they permitted to tell the world about it, when the apostle Paul wasn't?; (2) In mentioning his trip Paul stated that what he heard was inexpressible—he couldn't express it. Why then are the sights and sounds of today's heavenly trips not only expressible by a growing army of charismatic leaders but they are described in vivid detail, down to the color of heavenly grapes, grass, trees, and mansions—and even to the color of Christ's hair?

I have deliberately mentioned the perceived hair color of Christ by various visionaries throughout this book to underscore another point about contradictions among these stories. We've heard about golden locks, brown hair, and dark hair, but none of them have described seeing Jesus the same way the apostle John did when he received his vision on the Isle of Patmos. John also talked about being in heaven (although some scholars argue that it was a vision) and here was only part of his astounding description of Christ: "His head and hair were white like wool, as white as snow, and his eyes were like blazing fire" (Rev. 1:14). When one reads the rest of John's description of Christ the picture becomes almost, as Paul put it, inexpressible.

Additionally, Paul tells us that the experience was so profound that he was given a "thorn in the flesh" (perhaps it was a recurring illness; scholars are divided on it) so that he would not become puffed up with pride. But today's would-be visionaries don't suffer any maladies from their experiences, and in fact many of them teach that it is God's will for no believer to ever encounter sickness at all—it displays a lack of faith. I don't know a single case where any of them claim to have received a similar thorn in the flesh.

Heavenly Mansions

Although the "I went to heaven" stories don't match each other in significant ways, one commonality among

41

visionaries' pictures of heaven is that most talk about their seeing large mansions (which often resemble multi-roomed, Victorian, castle-like structures) being constructed for God's people in heaven. And although this might be justified on the basis of John 14:2 in which Jesus tells his disciples in the King James Version that "in my Father's house are many mansions . . . I go to prepare a place for you," a careful reading of the Greek wording in the passage reveals that there was little justification for translators to use the term "mansions," which denotes a worldly picture of a lavish house. According to *Vine's Expository Dictionary of New Testament Words* the Greek word *mone* is primarily a staying, an abiding, and it "denotes an abode," but was translated as "mansions" in the verse. The same Greek word was translated as "abode" in verse 23. "There is nothing in the word to indicate separate compartments in heaven; neither does it suggest temporary resting-places on the road."[26] Modern translations tend to translate verse 2 in a manner similar to the NIV: "In my Father's house are many rooms; if it were not so, I would have told you. I am going there to prepare a place for you."

But that still injects the "compartment" concept that is notably lacking in the original. A clearer paraphrase might be: "In my Father's world there are many places to abide, and to cease (not just rest from) your weary pilgrimage." Clearly, Christ's dominant thought is one of permanence, rootedness, and repose in heaven—not of any material circumstances that might go along with it. Any notion of "houses," with describable dimensions and furnishings, is completely beside the point. To elaborate something that is irrelevant is diversion by definition.

Last, when considering these stories we need to be aware of the possibility that they may ridicule and demean the real heaven that will some day be our home. Remember that heaven is the dwelling place of God, the Creator of the universe. Since we cannot fathom the wonders of our own world, much less determine the size of our own universe, how can we pretend to picture the next world?

We need to exercise discernment when we hear these stories. And we need to put them to the test of both logic and Scripture. If we carefully read the stories about heaven and the "Jesus" Betty Eadie allegedly saw, it was not the Jesus of the Bible, nor was it the entity that Hagin, Cho, Duplantis, Cerullo, or Liardon saw. And there are serious differences among the accounts of the latter five, although they are all prominent charismatic or Pentecostal leaders. Their heavens were contradictory, although some might argue that they were symbolic visions of the real thing.

We need to be aware of the fact that the Scriptures indicate that Satan is the father of lies and a deceiver who has been in business for a long, long time. In 1 Timothy 4:1, Paul talks about how in "later times some will abandon the faith and follow deceiving spirits and things taught by demons." We are told by the apostle John to "believe not every spirit, but try the spirits whether they are of God: because many false prophets are gone out into the world" (1 John 4:1 KJV).

I believe that these "Christs" allegedly being perceived by visionaries both inside the church and in the secular marketplace are not trustworthy in the least, and at worst are extremely dangerous. I believe they have caused some to abandon the faith and follow deceiving spirits.

We will put many of these tales to the test in the following chapters.

Writers of the Lost Realms

On July 31, 1959, something unusual happened to Betty Malz at the Terre Haute Union Hospital in Indiana. She claims that while she was there being treated for a ruptured appendix that eventually lapsed her into a forty-four-day coma, she died and found herself in heaven for twenty-eight minutes.

"The transition was serene and peaceful," she wrote in her best-selling book *My Glimpse of Eternity.* "I was walking up a beautiful green hill. It was steep, but my leg motion was effortless and a deep ecstasy flooded my body. Despite three incisions in my body . . . I stood erect without pain, enjoying my tallness, free from inhibitions about it. I looked down. I seemed to be barefoot, but the complete outer shape of my body was a blur and colorless."[1] Later, she said, she met Jesus in heaven (he looked like a bright light) before returning to her hospital bed as the result of her father's one-word prayer of "Jesus."

Malz's story first received notoriety in 1976 when well-known Christian writer Catherine Marshall published it in *Guideposts* magazine. The next year Chosen Books published *My Glimpse of Eternity,* which turned out to be the most popular Christian account of an alleged trip to heaven in recent times. The book not only launched Malz's career as a popular Christian author and conference speaker, it sold around one million copies and has been translated into eleven languages. She has gone on to write six other books, all of which mention her alleged trip to heaven. With her near-death experience forming the central plank of her message, she also landed appearances on Christian television and radio and has conducted women's retreats in forty-six states.

But in 1991 Christian writer Lorna Dueck, writing for the Canadian publication *ChristianWeek,* cast doubt on Malz's story.[2] Later other publications such as *Christianity Today* reported on the controversy.

In addition, this writer has learned that later accounts of her alleged experience *add to* her original account in *My Glimpse of Eternity.* For example, in *Angels Watching Over Me,* published ten years after her story first became known, she adds that she saw Jesus sitting on a "golden throne" and she "recognized people around the throne who had died during my lifetime, and they knew me,"[3] none of which were mentioned in *My Glimpse of Eternity.* And there are other apparent additions, some of which seem to contradict her original story in significant areas.

Arguably, one of the most popular "I went to heaven" (and hell) stories circulating through the church today also deserves scrutiny. It's the story of Dr. Richard Eby's alleged trips to heaven and hell. The primary problem with Eby's story is that there is evidence that he keeps adding new details when retelling it later. And sometimes the details contradict.

In *Caught Up into Paradise* Eby tells about how after a two-story fall on his head in 1972 he briefly died and was ushered into heaven where he had a "fantastic cloud-like body! . . . I was clothed in a translucent flowing gown, pure white, but transparent to my gaze. In amazement I could see through my body and note the gorgeously white flowers behind and beneath me."[4] He later came back to earth in a hospital room where Jesus assured him that he would be healed. Later the book relates, during a 1977 Trinity Broadcasting Network (TBN) tour to Israel when he was visiting Lazarus's tomb in Bethany, the lights went out and Jesus took him to hell:

> In the twinkling of an eye Jesus was standing beside me. . . . I heard the same wonderful Voice that had spoken to me from the cloud in my hospital room five years before:
> "My son; I showed you heaven, now I show you hell. You must know about them both . . ."[5]

"Praise the Lord for only two minutes of hell!" Eby wrote. "Even so, it was too long. . . . With terror came anger: hell-inspired curses flowed out in silence. My lips were silenced! Hate, wrath, cruelty, and insane rage rolled back and forth through me. Despite the utter silence I heard demons taunt me."[6] Eby then contradicted almost every other modern visionary claiming to have visited hell by stating that it is not a place of fire and flames. It's the opposite!

And then I noticed the cold. The kind that sickens and chills every cell just enough to ache but not get numb. There was no way ever to get warm, not in that dank pit! And the smell! Horrid, nasty, stale, fetid, rotten, evil . . . mixed together and concentrated. Somehow I knew instantly that these were the odors of my Pit-mates. Stinking, crawling, demons seen mentally delighting in making me wretched.[7]

Caught Up into Paradise didn't devote much space to Eby's heaven and hell visitations. But in subsequent books and speaking engagements Eby has added new, sensational details. He went on to claim that Jesus personally promised him that he would not die—he would be raptured with the church—his return was that close. Eby, born in 1912, is now 83.

More recently he diverged further from his original testimony of hell claiming on TBN that during his visit he heard music and witnessed demons there gyrating to heavy metal rock and roll "punk" music.

He furthered this claim in his 1991 book, *Didn't You Read My Book?* by giving new and contradictory information about his alleged visit to hell. In his first book, *Caught Up into Paradise,* Eby writes that during his visit to hell, the demons taunted him, and he screamed. "The clammy wet walls held me crushed for eternity without escape, without a Savior, without anything to maintain sanity!"

"*And then it was over,*" he writes (emphasis mine). "The lights flicked on [inside Lazarus's tomb when there was an apparent power outage]. The two ladies squealed with delight. Voices were laughing on the outside stairway" and he climbed out of the tomb and onto the tour bus.[8] But in his 1991 book Eby contradicts himself. He writes that after the demons taunted him suddenly he was *transported to heaven:*

Just in time I was lovingly snatched from this pit of Hell. I could have gone stark raving mad from terror had it lasted any longer. . . . Suddenly I was standing before the *Great White Throne* in awful terror. Obviously this was some portion of Heaven, but my fear mounted. I felt naked in body and soul and without a friend to plead my case. . . . Then Jesus again spoke to my mind: "As an unsaved sinner you are now before the Judgment Throne. You will witness the wages of sin."[9]

He was then taken to God the Father's presence, who was shrouded in mist. (He was not allowed to see God's face.) Out from the mist extended a hand "holding an *opened* Book," Eby wrote. He read in Hebrew the book's title inscribed in its back cover. It was the Lamb's Book of Life. He was told by the Voice from the Throne: "THIS IS *OUR* FAMILY ALBUM. YOUR NAME IS *NOT* IN IT. THERE IS ONLY ONE OTHER FAMILY—THE *FAMILY OF SATAN!* DEPART!" He was shown the "Lake of Fire"—a "galaxy-sized caldron of leaping flames" before being deposited back into Lazarus's tomb.[10]

Eby's descriptions of the demons and their rock and roll antics is especially colorful as it goes well beyond his original account—even giving us extended dialogue from their positions of being supervisors in hell.

Instantly I was in the center of the earth, the most indescribable plunge of terror that can be experienced. I was standing in a cavity in solid stone just large enough for me and a legion of demons. . . . With their fiery eyes fastened upon me, the one thousand spider-sized demons suddenly jumped away from my feet onto the side walls of this rock hole, racing up around my head. Their screaming taunts were audible upon my mind as separate voices, all declaring my profound stupidity in selecting hell instead of Heaven for the rest of eternity. Their constant shrieks of insane laughter over my plight were accented by their chants of AHA! AHA! AHA! (apparently a demonic AMEN!)[11]

"Deafening decibels of heavy-metal voodoo sounds" filled the cavern, Eby continued. These noises were "competing for loudness with the thousand voices of frenzied *rock and roll bodies* in epileptoid seizures" that taunted him. Later the demons confided in him: "Our boss, Satan, bound us in here just to keep you here and to make it hell for you. He taught us *rock-sex-music* to use around the world to *destroy* the kids. It works." . . . "Suddenly their invisible 'conductor' seemingly tapped his baton. The deafening heavy-rock beat began as the spider-chorus resumed its epileptoid convulsions of sexual writhings to obscene demonic language and laughter."[12]

Satan—In Charge of Hell?

In describing hell as a place where Satan and his hordes actually have any authority is an unscriptural premise. The Scriptures teach, whether talking about hell, Hades, tartarus, Gehenna, or other terms used to describe places of confinement or punishment after death, that Satan and his fallen angels will have no authority in those domains and will be left to their own punishment. In Matthew 25 when Jesus is talking about the final white throne judgment in heaven during which God the Father will separate the sheep from the goats, "he will say to those on his left, 'Depart from me, you who are cursed, into the eternal fire prepared for the devil and his angels.' . . . Then they will go away to eternal punishment, but the righteous to eternal life" (vv. 41, 46).

In 2 Peter 2 we are told that for some of the angels who sinned, he sent them "into gloomy dungeons to be held for judgment." (See also Jude 6.) Finally we read in Revelation that after the great tribulation an angel will seize Satan and bind him in "the Abyss" for a thousand years. Then after that Satan will be "thrown into the lake of burning sulfur, where the beast and the false prophet had been thrown. They will be tormented day and night for ever and ever" (20:2–10).[13]

Why, then, do we have so many persistent accounts that the realm of the damned is to be a place where demons are in control? Perhaps this stems from the thirteenth and fourteenth century when an influential book called *The Divine Comedy* by Dante captivated Europe. The book, which is still required reading in many modern literature classes, is a vivid satire. But it does picture hell as a place where demons and Satan himself are inflicting pain on the damned under their charge in hell.

Mary K. Baxter's Account

In Mary K. Baxter's *A Divine Revelation of Hell*, which has repeatedly appeared on the Christian best-seller lists, the author extensively pictures the devil and his angels as being in charge of hell. And she dramatically contradicts Eby's account. The book claims that Jesus took her on a forty-day personal tour of hell and later heaven in 1976. She claims hell is a place in the bowels of the earth where snakes slither about and rats scurry about. She adds that it is where people are burning but cannot die, even though worms are crawling through their ignited corpses.[14]

She also describes hell as being structured in the shape of a human—not like a small human-sized pocket in rock that Eby describes. It has a left and right leg, a belly, a heart, right and left arm, and a jaw, and each section of hell has slightly different torture chambers pocketed with many fiery pits. Baxter gives graphic accounts of demons and Satan himself inflicting more pain on people under their charge (29–31, 42). In one scene, demons are seen dancing around a coffin "chanting and laughing" as they keep thrusting spears into a human victim (51).

At the end of her book Baxter discloses her visions of heaven, contradicting virtually everyone else's. She claims that:

> . . . great billows of fire, bright lights and majestic power came before my eyes. In the center of the fire and the lights was the throne of God. . . . The air around the throne was filled with baby cherubim, singing and kissing the Lord upon His face, His hands and His feet. . . . The cherubim had tongues of fire sitting on their heads and on the tips of each tiny wing. The motion of their wings seemed synchronized with the movement of the power and glory of the Lord.[15]

Later, the book notes, she saw angels "busily cutting extremely large diamonds and placing them in the foundations of beautiful mansions" that are to be the homes of Christians (152).

The End-Time Handmaidens

There are certain Christians who are seemingly obsessed with visions of the other side and with accounts of devils roaming the stratosphere. Recently when I visited a church in the Philadelphia area, the pastor spoke of their weekly services in which he has to cast demons out from members of his own congregation (which I maintain is unbiblical). The pastor seemed preoccupied with sensational mystic tales and has invited numerous speakers into his church who have claimed to have been to the other side, including many mentioned in this book.

One of the most influential religious organizations preoccupied with heaven and hell are the End-Time Handmaidens of Jasper, Arkansas. The Handmaidens, a charismatic ministry headed by Gwen Shaw, carries in its stock at least twelve books about trips to heaven, some of which shoot wide of the biblical record of this realm in significant areas. In reprinting and distributing *Intra Muros* (meaning "Within the Gates"), which was originally published in 1898, the Handmaidens became culpable in spreading false doctrine because the book supports nineteenth century spiritualist ideas and the Mormon doctrine of eternal marriage between men and women in heaven.[16] *Intra Muros* is based on the nineteenth-century vision of heaven by Methodist Rebecca Springer (1832–1904).[17]

God's Word tells us—Jesus himself stated—that there will be no marriage in heaven, and in fact people will be "like the angels" (Matt. 22:30). *Intra Muros* also contradicts the biblical record in numerous other areas including the advocacy of works righteousness as a way of attaining heaven.

Another book reprinted by the End-Time Handmaidens in 1984 that was first published around the turn of the century is Elwood Scott's *Paradise: The Holy City and the Glory of the Throne*. This account is hard to take seriously due to its fanciful portrait of heaven as being a domain of flying horseless chariots (closely resembling futuristic George Jetson–type cars) flown about by angels and the saints. Each saint is supposedly given a harp to play. The book is permeated with ludicrous and racist thinking. For example, the book asserts that all Black people on earth *will become White in heaven*. But they won't lose their Black dialect of the English language—it will be spoken in heaven.

The main character in the book, Seneca Sodi, who claims to have spent forty days in heaven, gives an account of how he observed a group of singers in the distance and was told that "they were all colored people of America."[18] Drawing closer Sodi asks one of the singers, "Are there no black faces in heaven?" He is told: "We are all white here and in de perfect image of de Lord. . . . There's multitudes of dem here and dey sing in de choir wid de odder people and their voices are often de loudest."[19]

The End-Time Handmaidens also publish a thirteen-page testimonial booklet by Aline Baxley of California, who claims that after an automobile accident "the Death Angel carried me out to that outer darkness. I found myself in Hell, screaming, hollering, gnashing my teeth, begging the Death Angel not to leave me in Hell. Souls were around me by the hundreds and thousands, screaming and gnashing their teeth, just trying to die."[20] After God also showed her the lake of fire she woke up from a coma she'd been in for several days, so terrified that she asked Christ to save her from her sins.

The following is a summary of some of the tales circulating through the church (some of which are more fanciful than others). Notice how their descriptions seem to contradict each other, despite the fact that the originators of these stories all claim to be Christians, endowed with the Holy Spirit that the Bible calls the Spirit of truth (John 16:13).

- Percy Collett of Florida claims that he spent five and one-half days in heaven where he met and ate with guardian angels, and notes that "dogs in heaven do not bark, but the horses praise God."

In heaven "God the Father can be seen," he said. "He is bigger than Jesus and has feathers on his left hand."[21]

• Howard O. Pittman gives his account of the heavenly realm and the realm of demons in his book *Placebo* (which is based on his alleged near-death experience in 1979) and in *Demons: An Eyewitness Account.* In *Demons,* Pittman includes line drawings of the many different types of demons he was shown by the angels as they escorted him through the spirit world. Some appeared like frogs, he reported, while others looked like soldiers, mythological creatures, and a variety of other forms.

• The Sacramento-based organization, Advocate International Ministries, published the testimony of Irene Wakabi, a pastor in eastern Uganda who claims that when she was eleven years old in 1982, "a bright light fell from the sky" and in the center of the light was a group of singing angels. The light swooped down and picked her up and carried her off to "a place that looked like nothing that I had ever seen before that day." She said she felt as if she was standing on a "soft bright mattress which looked somewhat like the clouds and there seemed to be no sky." She saw golden streets, she said, and then was led to Jesus (who was wearing a white robe and whose "skin was bright and glorious") who taught her the Scriptures and ordained her. The same bright light then picked her up and deposited her back on earth.[22]

• In Ralph Wilkerson's 1977 book, *Beyond and Back,* he discusses various NDEs and "I went to heaven" stories. In Wilkerson's book, some of these types of stories seem credible, such as the experience of a woman who almost died following an airplane crash that killed her husband. Seconds after the crash she said she saw Jesus and he told her that her husband would be with him in eternity. "Jesus' face was one no artist could capture," the author writes. "His hair was a brownish auburn color, and it was to his shoulder. He wore a blue transparent robe over a lighter blue gown."[23]

- Perhaps one of the more plausible ones I've read involved the visions of Marietta Davis who fell into a nine-day trance in the summer of 1848 at her home in Berlin, N.Y. Upon awaking, she said that she had been in heaven and had also been shown hell. Although her story was first published in 1856, it has since been reprinted into at least thirty-six editions, including a recent edition published by Christ for the Nations, Inc., of Dallas and edited by that organization's founder, Gordon Lindsay, before his death. According to this edition called *Scenes Beyond the Grave,* when Marietta Davis returned to consciousness she accurately predicted the day of her death on the basis of her otherworldly revelations.[24] In her vision Jesus was adorned with a crown of pure light and had golden hair.[25] She also stated that in heaven the angels educate and instruct earthly infants and young children who have died before reaching an age of reason. But she too paints a picture of hell as a place of not only fire, but a domain of demonic revelry and laughter.[26]

Those tempted to believe any of the "I went to heaven or hell" stories need to consider some basic scriptural factors. The most obvious problem with these accounts, including the just mentioned nineteenth-century vision, is that there appears to be little scriptural evidence to support the assertion that the deceased are being tormented in a fiery place called hell at this time (although the Bible indicates they are undergoing punishment). In fact, hell, or Gehenna, may not yet exist—it is to be introduced into the future. According to Dr. Robert Morey's *Death and the Afterlife*: "The wicked *do not descend into Gehenna at death*, because it is the final place of punishment for the wicked after the resurrection,"[27] which has not yet occurred (emphasis mine).

Whom Can We Trust?

As we have seen, the words of the modern-day Christian travelers to heaven and hell are muddled at best, and outright lies at worst. Most, if not all, of the popular tales being distributed today along these lines fail the test of Scripture, in that they have gone beyond what is written.

This is not to say that some mystical experiences or the idea that those people may have caught a fleeting glimpse of God's power and majesty are all false. In the Old Testament there is the story of Elijah being transported to heaven in a fiery chariot in full view of Elisha. Ezekiel saw a strange vision reminiscent of Revelation 4, Moses descended from Mount Sinai with a glowing composure because he had spent time with God. Habermas and Moreland, in their book *Immortality: The Other Side of Death,* point out that hints of the same types of experience, not all of them detailing God's realm, may grace the New Testament:

. . . it is also at least possible that near-death phenomena are reported in Scripture. Stephen had a pre-death vision (Acts 7:55–56). Some think that the experience Paul describes in 2 Corinthians 12:1–5 occurred to him after he was stoned at Lystra and left for dead (Acts 14:19). In Jesus' story about the death of the poor man Lazarus, his post-death experience has similarities with some of the NDEs. . . . For that matter, the scenario in Luke 16:22–24 about the death of the rich man may remind us of some hellish near-death experiences.[28]

But today's accounts do not seem in many ways to be of the same variety as these biblical accounts. They seem to be self-serving. Brooks Alexander, of the Spiritual Counterfeits Project, writing about our culture's closely related fascination with angels, says that we shouldn't become preoccupied with seeking mystical experiences from the world beyond. "Let no one defraud you of your prize by delighting in self-abasement and the worship of angels, taking his stand on visions he has seen, inflated without cause by his fleshly mind," Alexander writes, quoting Colossians 2:17–18 NASB.

Paul clearly warns us not to seek such experiences, or to probe into the unseen realm. And the reason is equally clear: all such preoccupations only diminish the attention due to Christ. Christ and Christ alone is the fulcrum of God's saving work in history and the fountain of God's saving grace to man. We shouldn't give lesser claims the time of day, much less center stage.[29]

3

Embraced by the Darkness

Author Betty Eadie profited handsomely from her book about her trip to heaven. It has become a runaway best-seller with sales topping two million. Her story is that after undergoing a hysterectomy on November 18, 1973, at Riverton Hospital (now Highline Specialty Center) near Seattle, she hemorrhaged, died, and went to heaven. In heaven, she was literally embraced by Jesus Christ, who appeared as a bright light and imparted many "truths" to her.

Eadie has admitted to *People* magazine that she doesn't have any documentation about her hospital stay. "The exact length of time I was dead and whatnot were not documented, so I don't have those facts," she said.[1] However, even this information about her hospital stay has not been verified, because Betty Eadie has refused to make her hospital records public, throwing extra suspicion on her story. Further, she won't submit to hypnosis or to a polygraph test to verify the truthfulness of her experience, an experience that is trumpeted on the front cover as "the most profound and complete Near-Death experience ever."[2]

Eadie is inconsistent on other details as well. On ABC's *20/20* May 13, 1994, program (in which this author was featured giving his objections to the Eadie story) she said she did not want to give her doctor's name out of fear that it would injure his reputation. Then she said her doctor had died.

Watchman Fellowship's Craig Branch cited the irony with this:

> She claims that she doesn't want to get the doctor of the hospital in trouble even though the doctor is dead, and the hospital has changed owners.
>
> Eadie claims that "even if people get the proof, they won't accept it." This is a weak attempt at rationalization, and it makes her account look extremely suspect.[3]

In Richard Abanes's excellent book, *Embraced by the Light and the Bible: Betty Eadie and Near-Death Experiences in the Light of Scripture,* he gives us more reason to doubt her experience. He reports that in an early 1993 interview with Eadie, published just after the book's release, it states that Eadie's November 19, 1973, "death" at the hospital was "possibly up to two hours." But by mid-1993 Eadie was claiming she had died for nearly five hours.[4]

Branch comments on Eadie's premise: "It is hard to believe that after surgery she would have been left alone, even through a shift change, and that no one would have checked on her for over four hours."[5]

Perhaps this is a commentary on contemporary culture—it seems to not matter whether there is reason to doubt Eadie's story. Her story is so sensational and affirming of everyone—scoundrels of all sorts and dictators who led their peoples to ruin since the beginning of time all make it in the end without judgment in Eadie's "heaven." That seems to be the message that people want to hear. At one point her guides in heaven showed her a drunken man lying in a stupor on the sidewalk near a building. "Now we will show you who he really is," they told her.

> His spirit was revealed to me, and I saw a magnificent man, full of light. [Who, like Eadie and others in her scenario, had lived in heaven prior to his coming to earth to dwell in the body of that man.] Love emanated from his being, and I understood that he was greatly admired in the heavens. This great being came to earth as a teacher to help a friend that he had spiritually bonded with.[6]

But it would not be fair to explain away Eadie's success on her message alone. The book *is* well-written and easy to digest, full of vivid images of her alleged trip to heaven. And Eadie does mix her message with biblical truths. She talks about love being the most important quality people should strive for—something hard to take issue with in a world full of hate. After all, love, and the ability God gives us to love the unlovely for his sake, is a central theme in the Bible. "For God so loved the world, that he gave his only begotten Son . . ." the Bible declares in John 3:16 (KJV). And 1 John 4:8 declares that God is love.

But as I pointed out on the *20/20* show with Barbara Walters and Hugh Downs, God really is love. But that's only part of the picture. Jesus talked about judgment and hell about as much as he talked about heaven—sometimes in riveting detail. God is also just, and he judges all those who do not trust in his Son for salvation.

Embraced by the Light

The contradictions concerning some of the details in Eadie's near-death experience form the least of the concerns of evangelical Christians examining her story. It appears that Eadie has a lot to hide.

The Mormon Connection

The most important of these is the fact that Eadie is a Mormon and that many elements of the book openly promote Mormon doctrine, along with other ideas Bible-believing Christians would find objectionable. In addition, noted cult experts G. Richard Fisher and M. Kurt Goedelman of Personal Freedom Outreach say, *"Embraced by the Light* is a hodgepodge of Eastern mysticism, New Age philosophy, positive confession, Baha'i, Roman Catholicism, spiritism and a smattering of out-of-context Bible references."[7]

Some Christians are fooled into purchasing the book due to Eadie's claim to be a Christian who has dedicated the book to "The Light, my Lord and Saviour Jesus Christ, to whom I owe all that I have." Even though most Christian media outlets (radio, television, and magazines) have warned their readers that Eadie's book promotes Mormon doctrine, reports persist that some Christian bookstores continue to carry the book.

Even after running an article on the book's Mormon roots, *Charisma* magazine ran a letter to the editor supporting the book in its September 1994 issue. "Her story offers a loving Lord, full of the redemptive power revealed through His life, ministry and resurrection," it states. "Eadie clearly claims that although we are to respect other religions, there is fullness only through Jesus Christ and that there is no other way to God the Father except through Him. If people digest that one gospel truth, Eadie might be an instrument of God after all."[8]

However, the Jesus presented in the book is not the Jesus of the Bible, and her false Jesus endorses all ways as being channels to the Father. Consider these quotes from Eadie's January 3, 1994, appearance on the *Oprah Winfrey Show*.

Winfrey:	You know . . . what's fascinating to me . . . And I believe that there are many paths to God.
Eadie:	Yes.
Winfrey:	. . . many paths to the light . . . I certainly don't believe there is only one way. So did Jesus . . . You said the figure was Jesus?
Eadie:	Yes.
Winfrey:	Did Jesus indicate that to you?
Eadie:	Yeah . . . Absolutely.[9]

He is a false Jesus who told her according to an article in the March 6, 1993, Ogden, Utah, *Standard-Examiner* that the Church of Jesus Christ of the Latter-day Saints was "the truest Church on the earth."

There are many differences between Mormonism and Christianity, beginning with the nature of God himself, his revelation, his atonement on the cross outside Jerusalem two thousand years ago, and even his relationship to Satan. Mormonism teaches, for example, that

Lucifer (Satan) is the spirit brother of Jesus—which is blasphemous to Christians. Christians have always considered Mormonism's claim of human godhood over individual planets after death to be heresy. Indeed Mormonism and Christianity are not compatible.

Among those truths shown to Eadie, as documented by the *Christian Research Journal*,[10] that match Mormon beliefs were

- Pre-mortal existence. Eadie had realized that she and everyone else had lived prior to entering her earthly body.
- The necessity of the fall of man. She claims that Adam and Eve didn't have a "fall" in the Garden of Eden, but merely brought about conditions necessary for humankind's progression.
- A plurality of gods. Eadie teaches an eternal progression to godhead (45, 61, 109, 146) and declares that God the Father and Jesus are separate beings.
- Salvation after death. This of course is a prominent Mormon doctrine. But the Bible states that "it is appointed unto men once to die, but after this the judgment" (Heb. 9:27 KJV).

Abanes's book *Embraced by the Light and the Bible* exposes how Eadie's book is intertwined with Mormonism—both doctrinally and financially. At times it gives readers a line by line comparison of Eadie's book with the doctrines of Mormonism and the New Age movement. He also points out that Eadie's publisher, Gold Leaf Press of Placerville, California, "is the national marketing division of the Mormon-owned and operated Aspen Books of Murray, Utah," which is a publisher of Mormon works.[11] Abanes also points out that when the book was first released in the Utah area a special flyer entitled "Of Special Interest to Members of the Church of Jesus Christ of the Latter-day Saints" was inserted into the first several thousand copies of *Embraced by the Light* that were released in a predominantly Mormon section of Utah. It goes on to tell of Eadie's conversion to Mormonism and of her status as an active Temple Mormon who desires to convert others to the faith. Some evangelicals fear that the book has become a "Trojan horse" witnessing tool to bring non-Mormons into the Latter-day fold.

Yet, after the book was released nationally, Eadie and officials related to Gold Leaf Press have refused to confirm that fact or even list her religious affiliation—even under direct questioning. However, both Eadie's ward bishop in Seattle, Dan Miller, and LDS public relations manager Don LeFevre confirm that Eadie is an active Mormon.[12]

Other New Age Doctrine

It is also a well-known fact that *Embraced by the Light* promotes much New Age doctrine including mind-science "healing" and the Hinduistic doctrine of Monism—that we are one in substance with the universe.[13] Eadie has long been active in occultic circles, even becoming a popular New Age conference speaker. Spiritual Counterfeits Project's Warren Smith reports that during a July lecture in Milwaukee Eadie, "dressed in full Native-American garb," introduced herself as "On Jing Jinga" (rose in full blossom).

"She told everyone present that 'There is coming a time when you will not know who to turn to for spiritual direction. You need to turn to the pages of my book,' she said, reminding listeners that they were 'co-creators' with God . . . 'glorious beings of light' who have simply become mutated by those around us."[14]

Conflicting Stories

Still another criticism of Eadie is that she altered certain details of her story in a possible bid to be more palatable to the public, including affirming a belief system that accepts the practice of abortion. Eadie states that in heaven she was told that abortion is "contrary to that which is natural," and that a spirit waiting to come into a body suffers a sense of rejection when he or she is aborted. "That spirit," Eadie writes, "also feels compassion for its mother, knowing that she made a decision based on the knowledge she had."[15] Later when asked to be more specific by a publication, Eadie's executive assistant stated that Eadie believes abortion is "not a sin at all."

Once again Abanes unravels apparent deception from the Eadie camp. On the same page of an early edition of *Embraced by the Light* issued in Utah, the text is different; she speaks out against abortion! Abanes points out that it states:

> The spirit feels an immediate and devastating rejection. He knows that the body was to be his, whether it was conceived out of wedlock or was handicapped or was only strong enough to live a few hours; but now it has been taken from him. What happens to that spirit, or how it is healed, I don't know.[16]

Taking a Back Seat to Experience

Why, then, are so many people, some of them Christians, attracted to Eadie's message? Warren Smith gives us some clues. First, people don't want to believe the Bible. "In Eadie's scheme of things biblical truth always takes a back seat to spiritual experience," he wrote. "The gospel of her 'Jesus' bears little resemblance to scripture as it tickles people's ears and tells the human heart things it wants to hear."[17]

Eadie rejects the scriptural record of Jesus and claims that the Bible has been altered by man. "It is not an authority," she said. "Eadie had become a disciple of her New Age 'Jesus' . . . she had opened herself up to a 'broad way' Christianity that under the 'right' circumstances might one day become a global gospel,"[18] Smith said, adding:

> The bottom line in Betty Eadie's gospel is that the "broad way" will get you home. But that's not what Jesus says at all. He warns, "Enter ye in at the strait gate: for wide is the gate, and broad is the way, that leadeth to destruction, and many there be which go in thereat: Because strait is the gate, and narrow is the way, which leadeth unto life, and few there be that find it" (Matt. 7:13–14 KJV).[19]

Indeed the making of *Embraced by the Light* into a bestseller is disturbing in these last days—especially when one considers these serious contradictions. Perhaps it wouldn't matter as much if her book was trumpeted as a dream or clever fiction. But people are enthralled by her message—which has eternal consequences.

Saved by the Light

Since the unprecedented success of *Embraced by the Light,* which has remained on the best-seller list for more than a year, other copycat books have been rolling out of publishing houses.

By far the most successful of these has been Dannion Brinkley's *Saved by the Light,* which has also reached the top ten on the *New York Times* best-seller list. Brinkley too has appeared on dozens of the nation's top talk shows and has had incredible media coverage.

Eadie's book, a toxic mix of New Age teachings and mind-science theology, sprinkled with a dose of Mormonism, has overshadowed the heresies in Brinkley's book. Few evangelicals have tackled the ideas put forth in the Brinkley best-seller. But an analysis of *Saved by the Light* reveals that it could be even *more* lethal to one's soul than Eadie's book.

Like Eadie's work, Brinkley's book contains an overt Mormon connection. Brinkley writes that the Mormon Church has collected many accounts of NDEs in the *Journal of Discourse* (a commentary on Mormon beliefs), and states that "their findings match everything that happened to me. My guess is that these beliefs were derived from personal experiences," he writes. "Many of the Mormon elders have had near-death experiences or gathered detailed accounts of them from fellow churchgoers. . . . Death for instance, is defined as 'merely a change from one status or sphere of existence to another.'"[20] Brinkley also speaks of Mormonism later, and notes that "Mormons did not make near-death experiencers feel crazy. Since the afterlife was a part of their church doctrine, they actually welcomed testimony on what had been seen and heard on the other side" (105, 106). He also, like Eadie, affirms the Mormon doctrine of the preexistence of souls (81).

But, unlike Eadie, who dedicated her book to "The Light, my Lord and Saviour Jesus Christ," Brinkley's book portrays a heaven *without Jesus Christ*—he is not present, and it is a place where all paths eventually lead. "All people should be free to worship the way they choose," Brinkley concludes. "There are many paths to righteousness" (160).

In the place of God the Father or Jesus his Son, in Brinkley's "heaven," were thirteen beings of light "as though each one represented a different sign of the zodiac" (29). (Although there are twelve signs of the zodiac, Brinkley states that the thirteenth being was a bit more powerful than the first twelve who emanated the emotions of the zodiac.)

But while Jesus is not mentioned in Brinkley's "heaven," he does affirm the universalism Eadie promoted in her book—that all roads lead to God and that everyone makes it in the end. However, biblical Christianity teaches a narrow and exclusive way of salvation, a way affirmed in biblical passages such as John 14:6, where Jesus declares to be "the way, the truth, and the life: *no man cometh unto the Father, but by me*" (KJV, emphasis mine).

Brinkley also repeats the original lie of the Garden of Eden in stating that humanity is God (127) and that human beings have "gone to earth to co-create with God" (45).

Dannion Brinkley is a close friend of Dr. Raymond Moody, who grandfathered the NDE phenomenon with the publication of his 1975 book, *Life after Life*. Brinkley says he received his revelations about heaven during two NDEs. The first came in 1975 when he was talking on the phone during a thunderstorm and a bolt of lightning hit the phone line, sending thousands of volts of electricity into his body, stopping his heart. His second experience came in 1989 when his heart gave out during an illness. In each case he claims to have traveled to a crystal city where angelic instructors taught him many new truths and imparted psychic powers to him, such as the ability to read minds and predict future events. His forecasts include that "environmentalism would emerge as the world's new religion" and that soon America would cease to be a world power due to "two horrendous earthquakes."[21]

To discerning Christians the most troubling aspect of Brinkley's message is that it leads to things contrary to God's Word, and from there into the dangers of the occult. The thirteenth being he allegedly met told him his purpose on earth: "You are there to create spiritualistic capitalism. You are to engage this coming system by changing people's thought processes. Show people how to rely on their spiritual selves instead of the government and churches. Religion is fine, but don't let people be entirely controlled by it."[22]

Upon his return to earth Brinkley said he began to fulfill that mission by building centers where people can learn to use their psychic powers, such as the ability to communicate with spirits, including the spirits of the deceased—which is specifically forbidden in Scripture. Moody, as Brinkley disclosed in his book (158) and in a recent television interview with Diane Sawyer, has also diverted much of his attention these days to communicating with the dead. Some Scripture verses condemning this practice are Exodus 22:18; Leviticus 19:31; Deuteronomy 18:10–11; 1 Samuel 28:3; 1 Chronicles 10:13; Isaiah 8:19; Acts 16:16–18; Galatians 5:19–21; 1 Timothy 4:1–2; and Revelation 22:15.

Brinkley implies that sheer mind power can heal physical ailments, a belief of the mind-science cults (156).

There is also no hell in Brinkley's alleged glimpses of the other side. The first time he died, a being of light reviewed his life and showed him that he was a "truly worthless person" who had not cared about his fellow human beings. However, the being exuded a "nonjudgmental compassion" for him (20).

It is possible Dannion Brinkley met a being of light. But it was not God or one of God's angels in heaven. The apostle Paul warns of Satan being able to transform himself into an angel of light (2 Cor. 11:14). We need to test all things and hold fast to that which is true. *Saved by the Light* does not meet this standard of truth about salvation, God, or the afterlife.

One with the Light

Prolific New Age/UFO writer Brad Steiger (a.k.a. Eugene Olson, originally from Decorah, Iowa) jumped into the fray with the September 1994 publication of *One with the Light* in which he even outdoes Brinkley in advocating spiritism. Steiger concludes the book, which is jam-packed full of stories of people who have passed over to the other side to witness "the light," with a "how-to-do-it" exercise in visualization that will help the reader become one with the light and help meet his or her spirit guide!

"For superior results," instructs Steiger, "I suggest that you prerecord the following exercises in your *own* voice, then play the tape back so that you can serve as your own guide. . . . If you should fall into an altered state of consciousness . . . you will simply awaken within a brief time."[23]

Later in the exercise, Steiger equates seeing a light while in an altered state as meeting one's "spiritual guide" or "guardian angel," and he encourages his readers to allow that "angel guide" to bring the individual into "the heavenly kingdom" without an NDE![24] Through guided imagery the reader can go to heaven and be "clothed in a robe of white with a golden cord tied around your middle," Steiger writes. "And look ahead. *See the beautiful crystal kingdom!*"[25] He then uses three pages to describe the sights and wonders of heaven and takes us into "the great door of the Temple of Love, Wisdom, and Knowledge" and directly before a golden altar into the "Holy of Holies" itself. And although Steiger talks a lot about Christ in *One with the Light,* Jesus or any part of the Holy Trinity of God (the Father, the Son, and the Holy Spirit) are nowhere to be seen in his heaven.

What we do read about Jesus throughout the book is contrary to God's Word. He talks about the supposed importance of having divine love (44, 193), but there is nothing in the book about his (Christ's) atoning death on the cross. Instead Steiger's book is a survey of participants, whose stories affirm many roads to God (50), including reincarnation (261), Zen Buddhism (277, 286), Native American shamanism, Shirley MacLaine and the New Age movement (277), the Indian Bhagavad-Gita (288), and numerous other false religious concepts. And to top it off, he concludes the book with a quote that *denies death itself* from "the great Yogi and mystic Parmahansa!"[26]

Death is real, and the Bible has a lot to say on the topic. And it does not affirm reincarnation. "He [God] remembered that they were but flesh," the psalmist writes, "a passing breeze that does not return" (Ps. 78:39).

I believe in visions and I believe God has, at times, given people glimpses of his glory. One person God disclosed many secrets to, including the promise of eternal life, was the Old Testament prophet Daniel. This great man, held in exile in Babylonia at about 605 B.C., was given a panoramic view of the history of the nations. Daniel was told that at the end times, following "a time of distress such as has not happened from the beginning of nations," that his people—"everyone whose name is found written in the book—will be delivered." But there will be a judgment, and there will be a hell. Not everyone makes it in the end as Steiger, Eadie, Brinkley, and a score of other NDEers are affirming. "Multitudes who sleep in the dust of the earth will awake," Daniel was told, "some to everlasting life, others to shame and everlasting contempt" (Dan. 12:1–2).

A Different Jesus

Why are so many people today claiming to have NDEs? Why are so many people claiming to have revelations of Jesus in heaven that clearly contradict each other and the record we have in Scripture? I believe it could be because we may very well be nearing the time of unprecedented distress that Daniel refers to.

If we look at the scriptural record referring to the end times, the Bible teaches that there will be a time of great religious deception just prior to Jesus' coming and the setting up of his kingdom. In Matthew 24:5 Jesus gave this warning: "Many will come in my name, claiming, 'I am the Christ,' and will deceive many." Furthermore he said, "At that time many will turn away from the faith and will betray and hate each other, and many false prophets will appear and deceive many people." (See also Matt. 24:10, 11.) Finally, Jesus warned them about religious deception:

> At that time if anyone says to you, "Look, here is the Christ!" or, "There he is!" do not believe it. For false Christs and false prophets will appear and perform great signs and miracles to deceive even the elect—if that were possible. See, I have told you ahead of time.
> So if anyone tells you, "There he is, out in the desert," do not go out; or, "Here he is, in the inner rooms," do not believe it.
>
> Matthew 24:23–26

Today we not only have false Christs appearing in ashrams and operating in religious cults worldwide in places such as Waco, Texas; Jonestown, Guyana; Korea, and in a multitude of other places on this planet. We have false, counterfeit Christs presented in New Age fairs, on television talk shows . . . and in best-selling books, tickling the ears of the masses.

May God help us, as he says, to convince people to "not believe it!"

Near-Death
Experiences, Spiritism,
and the Occult

It is not surprising that Brad Steiger's book *One with the Light* heads directly into the world of the occult. Steiger is teaching spiritism—communicating with spirits, which is akin to what has come to be popularly known as channeling.

Almost all of the early pioneers of modern-day research into NDEs were avid occultists who had reached their conclusions about the other side after becoming deeply involved in occult practices. They were also influenced greatly by each other, and sometimes by other occultists and their sources. Although these facts are not common knowledge to the public, the occult/New Age press has reported on it for a long time, along with a small number of astute evangelical Christian writers often connected with cult-watching organizations.

The word *occult* literally means "things hidden or secret." Biblically, to dabble in the occult is strictly forbidden by God in his Word. Occult practices include astrology, dowsing, tarot cards, fire walking, witchcraft, fortune-telling, palm reading, magical arts, ouija boards, parapsychology and ESP, numerology, cabala, pyramidology, crystal ball reading, spiritism, mediumship and channeling, and a host of other practices. The New Age movement is a quasi-Hinduistic movement whose practitioners often engage in many of these occult practices.

Trafficking with spirits, whether they be supposed space aliens,[1] ghosts, disembodied spirits, deceased ancestors, or unknown voices or influences in the cosmos, is called necromancy. In God's Word it is also known as witchcraft or sorcery. As we will see, all of the most influential pioneers in the field—Dr. Raymond Moody, Dr. George Ritchie, Elisabeth Kübler-Ross, and Robert Monroe—were associated with each other. And all had consulted with "familiar spirits" and/or alleged spirits of the dead.

Spiritism, Channeling, and Mediumship

Let us better define our terms. In occult circles today there is sometimes a division between mediums and channelers. New Age writer Jon Klimo, quoting California parapsychologist D. Scott Rogo, writes:

> Mediumship is the art of bringing through spirits of the dead specifically to communicate with their rela-

tives. Channeling I define as bringing through some sort of intelligence, the nature undefined, whose purpose is to promote spiritual teaching and philosophical discussion.[2]

Channeling and mediumship can also be done in a number of ways, but among the most popular of these are through "trance or sleeping channeling/mediumship" and "automatic writing."[3]

Let's look at some of the Bible's warnings against channeling. The prophet Isaiah, writing about 2,700 years ago, gave this word from the Lord:

> And when they shall say unto you, Seek unto them that have familiar spirits, and unto wizards that peep, and that mutter: should not a people seek unto their God? for the living to the dead?
>
> Isaiah 8:19 KJV

The passage then goes on to say that there is no light in them and that they will fall under judgment—even to the point of being "driven to darkness" (vv. 20–22). In Exodus 22:18 God tells Moses that he should not allow a witch to live. Leviticus 19:31 says this: "Regard not them that have familiar spirits, neither seek after wizards, to be defiled by them: I am the LORD your God" (KJV). In the next chapter God states that he will cut himself off from his people who practice spiritism (20:6). Deuteronomy 18:10 is also stern: "There shall not be found among you any one that . . . useth divination . . . or an enchanter, or a witch."

An Old Testament Example

King Saul was judged by God because he tried to consult with the spirit of Samuel, who had been dead, and that was the reason he lost his crown and suffered a wretched death. In that case, Saul consulted with a witch who agreed to try to bring up the spirit of Samuel to bring him advice. But instead of the witch bringing up a familiar spirit *to pose as Samuel,* God, in judgment, allowed the *real* Samuel to come back and pronounce God's wrath on him. Even the witch was terrified to see the real spirit of Samuel arrive on the scene. "So Saul died . . . for asking counsel of one that had a familiar spirit," the Bible says, summarizing the story in 1 Chronicles 10:13 (KJV).

I brought out this point to illustrate the fact that this incident (along with Jesus on the mountain of transfiguration conversing with Moses and Elijah)[4] are the only recorded conversations between the living and the dead—*and it was only through God's supernatural intervention that it happened.* The Bible tells us that this type of communication is *impossible* through human or occult means. In Jesus' parable of the rich man and Lazarus (Luke 16:19–31), the rich man who is suffering in hell asks Abraham if he can return to earth and warn his five brothers about the torments to come. His request is denied: "If they hear not Moses and the prophets, neither will they be persuaded, though one rose from the dead," Abraham says (v. 31 KJV).

Familiar Spirits in the New Testament

In the Book of Acts as God was launching the early church via signs and wonders, more of the powers behind the scene were detailed when sorcerers and mediums were placed under judgment for their evil acts. Simon the sorcerer was rebuked by Peter in Acts 8:9–24, and Paul struck Elymas the sorcerer blind in Acts 13:6–12. Paul cast a demon who gave the power to have communication with familiar spirits out of a medium/channeler in Acts 16:16–18. Later in 1 Timothy, Paul links so-called revelations from spirits directly with doctrines of demons (4:1 KJV) and states that in the latter times "some shall depart from the faith, giving heed to seducing spirits." In 2 Corinthians 11:14, Paul tells us that Satan is capable of transforming himself into an angel of light. This is especially interesting in light of the fact that nearly every NDEer reports meeting a being of light.

So, although talk shows are abuzz with channelers going into trances and bringing messages from the other side, and books such as the *Urantia Book* and *A Course in Miracles* are the rage today, these practices are so serious to God that they can affect one's eternal destiny. The apostle Paul, writing in the Book of Galatians, tells us that those that practice the works of the flesh "will not inherit the kingdom of God" (5:21b). Listed as one of the works is witchcraft. The apostle John, who was shown a heavenly vision, tells us that the "fearful, and unbelieving, and the abominable, and murderers, and whoremongers, *and sorcerers,* and idolaters, and all liars, shall have their part in the lake which burneth with fire and brimstone: which is the second death" (Rev. 21:8 KJV, emphasis mine).

Connections with Spiritism and the Occult

Betty Eadie

There is evidence that Betty Eadie, though more veiled about her past, has also been involved with the occult. Eadie is a licensed hypnotherapist, a profession often linked to the occult, and has had her own practice until perhaps as late as March 1993.[5] Eadie also affirms her belief in all living things, even plant life, as having "auras,"[6] which is a concept from the occult. She has also admitted to having spirit guides that she calls "guardian angels" appear to her on occasion. On the *Oprah Winfrey Show* she called them "spiritual beings" and said three of them appeared in her room.[7]

But these are relatively mild when compared with the trafficking in spirits of those who have gone before her.

Elisabeth Kübler-Ross

In September 1976, Dr. Elisabeth Kübler-Ross made an incredible confession to a crowd of 2,300 who had gathered to hear her speak: "Last night I was visited by Salem, my spirit guide, and two of his companions, Anka and Willie," she said. "They were with us until three o'clock in the morning. We talked, laughed and sang together. They spoke and touched me with the most incredible love and tenderness imaginable. This was the highlight of my life."[8]

Albrecht and Alexander, writing in the April 1977 *SCP Journal,* comment on her admission:

> There are several things to note in this account. The first is that what is described here can only be classified as a form of concourse with the forbidden spiritual realm [necromancy] and therefore bears the full weight of the relevant biblical warnings and judgments. The second point is that the *quality* of the manifestations Dr. Kübler-Ross speaks of are characteristic of a deep and prolonged involvement with spiritistic practices. Sustained, external, public displays by spirit beings do not normally occur unless there has been a considerable belief-commitment and surrender of will to the spirit[s] involved.[9]

At the time Kübler-Ross, a Swiss-born psychiatrist, had gained worldwide fame for her pioneering work in the field of thanatology—the study of death. She had spent ten years researching death and the emotional problems of terminal patients and had done groundbreaking work helping to document the stages of dying.

But prior to that time she became interested in other aspects of the topic, including what happens following death. That led her to the research of Dr. Raymond Moody, who had been schooled in the deep things of spiritism by two others, Dr. George Ritchie and Robert Monroe. Eventually Kübler-Ross became so entwined with Moody's work that she often spoke on his behalf at his lectures, and she wrote the foreword to his book, *Life after Life*.

Monroe, author of *Journeys Out of the Body*, helped Kübler-Ross have her first out-of-body experience at his Virginia-based Monroe Institute for Applied Science during an occult meditation experiment. Later she continued having occult experiences, which led her to contact many "spirit guides." In a 1977 *Human Behavior* article about Kübler-Ross, her main guide, Salem, was described as a "handsome Egyptian-looking man with a brownish face and hairy arms."[10] Eventually Kübler-Ross became involved in other occultic forays, including past life regression.

Robert Monroe

In *Journeys Out of the Body*, Monroe touches on truly bizarre elements of occultism and necromancy. According to Albrecht and Alexander, Monroe claims in the book to have had numerous paranormal experiences with dead persons including "out-of-the-body trysts and disembodied sexual encounters."[11] This eventually led to his forming an organization that he named "M–5000." The sole purpose of the organization is to help facilitate out-of-body experiences for clients like Kübler-Ross, who has served on the board of advisors.

Tal Brooke, president of the Spiritual Counterfeits Project, was personally acquainted with Robert Monroe, Dr. George Ritchie, and fellow student Raymond Moody while he was an undergraduate at the University of Virginia in Charlottesville in the late 1960s. Following college, Brooke traveled to India to follow Eastern yogis and eventually became super guru Sai Baba's top Western disciple. Disillusioned with the deception of the East, and astounded by the power and love of Jesus Christ, he became a Christian in 1971, settled back in the States, and wrote a book (that was eventually banned in India) exposing Sai Baba as a false prophet.[12]

Brooke cites Monroe with using technology through sophisticated tape and meditation techniques in order to produce mediumship.[13] He writes in *The Other Side of Death* that he remembers helping Monroe with his out-of-body experiments:

> I unwittingly found myself working with Monroe on the tape prototypes that eventually would become the M–5000 program, a complex, multichannel recorded tape which would be used across the country to induce astral experiences in the uninitiated. [14]

Raymond Moody

According to Brooke, Raymond Moody, the famous author of *Life after Life,* had long been involved in spiritism prior to his research in NDEs, and he was intently involved in occultic topics. But only a glimmer of this came through in his book when he quoted

The Tibetan Book of the Dead and the writings of the eighteenth-century mystic Emanuel Swedenborg.

According to the *SPC Journal,* Brooke and Moody were friends at the University of Virginia in the late 1960s, and Moody tried to influence him there on spiritual things.

> Moody claimed that he regularly conversed with a spirit being (which he identified as "God") who manifested primarily as a voice in his head. A favorite topic of conversation between Moody and his spiritual mentor was the positioning and arrangement of flowers on the University campus (even at the time, Brooke says, this struck him as an odd topic of divine concern).[15]

Their friendship gravitated around the occult, Brooke said. But in the early years of his success, Moody's work appeared to be an objective, scientific work documenting NDEs, and he even portrayed himself as a Methodist Christian. The result of this had been acceptance of his NDE message, initially, by a number of undiscerning Christians, and worse yet, by pastors trumpeting Moody's message to their congregations.

But in the 1980s, Moody's true belief system strongly emerged. He became a popular speaker at many New Age and occult events. And as illustrated in his 1993 book entitled *Reunions: Visionary Encounters with Departed Loved Ones,* Moody's interest has geared away from a scientific basis of objective analysis into a subjective preoccupation with communicating with spirits of the dead. Abanes points out (as illustrated in a recent prime time television show with ABC's Diane Sawyer) that the methods Moody uses are not scientific at all; they are akin to crystal ball readings. His collection of mirrors in the attic of his retirement home in Alabama through which he claims he can contact the dead is called "skrying" and it is "a very old form of divination."[16] Through this method, he reports in *Reunions,* Moody has been able to contact his grandmother.

Dr. George Ritchie

Moody's interest in the field of NDEs came as the result of a compelling story told by his friend, psychiatrist Dr. George Ritchie, who claimed he died in 1943 for a short time in Barkley, Texas. Moody, who dedicated *Life after Life* to Ritchie, was so impressed by Ritchie's story that he began his lifelong quest to investigate NDEs.

According to Ritchie's book *Return from Tomorrow* (Chosen, 1978), while in an army hospital suffering from pneumonia-like symptoms, he died and found himself out of his body and able to fly through the skies over earth. Later he met Jesus who showed him various spiritual realms before he reentered his body and recovered from his illness. His otherworldly perspective changed him forever, he wrote, as he realized that Jesus, a being of light, was trying to teach him the importance of unconditional love.

Return from Tomorrow reads like an evangelical Christian book in many ways. It doesn't contain anything overtly cultic or many things that are absolutely unbiblical. It was cowritten by Elizabeth Sherrill, who also coauthored such best-selling Christian books as *The Cross and the Switchblade, The Hiding Place,* and *God's Smuggler.* Ritchie dedicates the book to the late Christian writer Catherine Marshall "who first insisted I tell it all." The book also received a "Mark of Excellence" award from *Campus Life,* an influential Christian magazine.

However, Ritchie is deeply involved in occultism, even conducting seminars in conjunction with followers of Edgar Cayce (1877–1945), founder of the Association for Research and Enlightenment (ARE), based in Virginia Beach. Ritchie has gone on to pen another book called *My Life after Dying,* in which he affirms universalism, reincarnation, spiritism, and other doctrines anathema to Christians. Ritchie's views are now very New Age. Does this mean that Ritchie, who sounds like a born-again Christian in *Return from Tomorrow,* has apostatized? Has he left the Christian faith?

Hardly, according to Tal Brooke. Ritchie's occultic views were well-known in the early 1970s.[17] Brooke reports in *The Other Side of Death* that at a retreat in Massanetta Springs, Virginia, in 1972 (following Brooke's return from India), Ritchie disclosed that God told him in 1958 that sixty-thousand "mother ships of UFOs" were soon going to sweep down upon planet earth to pick up the "remnant of true believers on the earth before our planet is plunged into darkness and catastrophe."[18]

"Ritchie was informed that he was the new Noah of this age and that the vehicles used would be flying saucers," Brooke wrote, adding that he realized that Ritchie was a deceiver.[19] It's quite natural then that Ritchie would wind up with Cayce's organization.

Edgar Cayce

Cayce, often called the sleeping prophet, was a trance channeler who taught reincarnation and astrology. As a boy, he claimed to have seen apparitions and "little people" or "play folk" appear to him.

As I wrote in my last book, *UFOs in the New Age,* Cayce was also a false prophet who during his fourteen-thousand "readings" (trance channeling sessions that were transcribed) claimed that the lost continent of Atlantis could rise from the ocean floor in the twentieth century. Cayce propounded:

> metaphysical "truths" that included a new, unbiblical view of Jesus, reincarnation, gnosticism, astrology, monism, and Atlantis. These "truths" were not always true. For example, he predicted that New York City would sink into the ocean in the 1970s.[20]

On Jesus, Cayce claims to have gone back in time via "the universal mind" to reveal the hidden years of Christ's life. Cayce claims that Jesus, a "perfect master," learned his magical miracle-working abilities (including healing, weather control, and telepathy) first in Egypt, then from holy men in India and Tibet. He then returned to Palestine as the Messiah.[21]

A Pattern of Deception

Ritchie's Jesus matches Moody's Jesus, and in many ways they match Eadie's Jesus, too, although their descriptions of the heaven and other realms don't always agree. But their Jesus is similar in the sense that he says little or *nothing* about sins and the need for a Savior. All of these accounts are utterly false presentations of the Christ of the Bible. They are, as the apostle Paul describes in 2 Corinthians 11:4, presentations of "another Jesus" contrary to the one of history.

In Galatians 1:6–9 Paul warns against following "another gospel" with one that would upset their faith.

> Though we, or an angel from heaven, preach any other gospel unto you than that which we have preached unto you, let him be accursed.

As we said before, so say I now again, If any man preach any other gospel unto you than that ye have received, let him be accursed (KJV).

There is also another commonality to almost all the books written today on the afterlife, including works by those mentioned in this chapter. They try to "unify the biblical and occult tradition and say that they both reveal the same truth and that both point to the same god."[22]
That is a diabolical deception.

What Is Death, Anyway?

espite the fact that Moody, Elisabeth Kübler-Ross, and others were deeply involved with the occult as they were researching NDEs in the early days, some have argued that Moody did important work in the field by illustrating common experiences people were having during their NDEs. And perhaps there is something to be said for Moody bringing the concept of death—even helping us to think more of our own inevitable deaths—to the forefront of popular culture during the late 1970s.

The same, perhaps, can be said for Kübler-Ross's work with terminal patients. Her analysis of the death process is said to have helped bring comfort to many people grappling with the imminent death of loved ones.

Indeed, Moody's work has lasted. Today in the mid-1990s, almost everyone is familiar with his research and the fifteen elements he lists as common to NDEs. Thanks to his work, almost *everyone* has heard about meeting a "bright light" after going down a tunnel following death.

Moody's work was fascinating, and as a young Christian in the 1970s, I became extremely intrigued after reading *Life after Life*.

Common Elements of NDEs

Let us take a look at the fifteen elements common to NDEs as cited by Moody. Not everyone who claimed to have had an NDE experienced all fifteen elements. The wording describing each element has been taken from Jerry Isamu Yamamoto's excellent two-part series on NDEs that appeared in the spring and summer 1992 *Christian Research Journal*:[1]

1. Ineffability

Many of those who have experienced an NDE say that no words can adequately or truly describe what happened to them. The experience, for them, is inexpressible.

2. Hearing the News

Many of them related hearing a medical person pronounce them dead. To those around them, all their bodily signs indicated that they had expired, but during that moment, they consciously knew they were still alive.

3. Feelings of Peace and Quiet

Many people recall feeling sensations of extreme pleasure. Although severe pain normally accompanies a life-threatening injury or disease, they remember feeling only a deep peace and quietness during the NDE.

4. The Noise

Many relate hearing a distinct sound that occurs either at or near death. In some cases, this noise can be quite pleasant, like rapturous music. In other cases, the noise can be harsh and disturbing, like continuous buzzing or banging.

5. The Dark Tunnel

Many recollect being jerked through some dark passageway, frequently while hearing the noise. This dark tunnel has been variously described as a cave, a sewer, a trough, a valley, and so on.

6. Out of the Body

Many remember seeing their physical bodies apart from themselves as though they were "spectators" observing their bodies. Surprise, panic, and a desire to return to their bodies often accompanied the realization that they were separate from their physical form.

7. Meeting Others

In many cases they encountered spiritual entities who were present to help them through the experience. These beings variously appeared as loved ones who had recently passed away, strangers who had died, or some other spirits who were acting as their guardians.

8. The Being of Light

Quite a few speak of beholding a brilliant light that, despite its brilliance, did not hurt their eyes. To them, this radiant light was a personal being who emanated irresistible love and warmth and who communicated with them—through thoughts and not speech—about the meaning of their lives.

9. The Review

A number of them recall an instant moment of time during their experience in which they witnessed a vivid review of their lives. These panoramic images provoked in them the importance of loving people and under-standing the meaning of life.

10. The Border or Limit

Some recount being obstructed by some form that often prevented them from going any further in their journey or from reaching that being of light. It can be a fence, a door, a body of water, or even an imaginary line.

11. Coming Back

All of them obviously returned from their near-death experience, but how they felt about coming back varies considerably. Some wanted to stay with the being of light. Others felt obliged to return to complete unfin-ished tasks. Some chose to return. Others were told to come back. In any case, the return is often instanta-neous—back through the dark tunnel.

12. Telling Others

Those who have had NDEs regard their experience as a real event rather than a dream. But since they believe that it was extraordinarily unique and that others would be skeptical, they are quite reticent about disclosing their experience, which they feel is inexpressible anyway.

13. Effects on Lives

As profound as the effects of their NDEs were on them, none feel that the experience has perfected them, and few have tried to gain public attention because of it. Instead, the effects have been more in the way they now view life and regard others. As was mentioned earlier, caring for other people and gaining a better understanding of the meaning of life emerged as high priorities after their experience.

14. New Views of Death

Most of them no longer fear physical death, but at the same time they do not seek it. Rather, they view death as a transitional state to another form of life. Entrance into this new life involves neither judgment nor the dispensing of rewards and punishments.

15. Corroboration

Remarkably there are independent testimonies of people who have corroborated some of the details in NDE accounts; that is, specific incidents (e.g., in the hospital operating room) witnessed by those who were supposedly dead. Although their testimonies do not constitute proof of life after death, they are significant considerations in the study of NDEs.

Medical Explanations

Some have argued that these experiences can be attributed to medical and other scientific causes. Others have claimed they are elaborate hoaxes, products of overactive imaginations. Why, for instance, doesn't everyone whose heart stops beating or whose breathing stops (many times for periods longer than those reporting NDEs) experience at least some of Moody's stages? Many recall nothing at all.

One of the most popular alternative explanations is elaborated on by psychologist Susan Blackmore, author of *Dying to Live*. Blackmore has been a guest on various programs, including the *20/20* show, trying to make sense of Betty Eadie's story. "In her mind she saw Jesus because that's what she expected to see, because that's what she wanted to see, but she interpreted it as real," Blackmore said. "I would interpret it as hallucination."[2]

Blackmore wasn't necessarily attributing dishonest motives to Eadie. What she meant was that when an individual stops receiving oxygen, things start to happen to the brain and other organs. It's known as *hypoxia,* and some believe it can cause hallucinations, pleasurable feelings, and a natural high in an NDE.[3]

Yamamoto lists other alternative explanations, including hallucinations caused by narcotics and recreational drugs, as well as drugs and anesthetic agents often used on hospital patients who later experience an NDE.

Four other possible explanations Yamamoto gives us are *autoscopic hallucinations, the endorphin model, transient depersonalization,* and *memories of birth.*

Autoscopic hallucinations is a psychological "event of seeing one's double," according to Yamamoto, adding that it is often associated with brain tumors, strokes, and migraine headaches. In these conditions persons will often superimpose his or her double on reality.

In the *endorphin model,* Yamamoto writes that in times of sudden stress and/or pain, the body produces a large amount of endorphins, which are natural chemicals to relieve pain or stress. It is possible that this creates pleasurable and mystical high feelings. *Transient depersonalization* is related in the sense that instead of "natural chemicals reacting to the stress of dying, a psychological mechanism is triggered in response to this stress to create a sense of separation from the prospect of physical annihilation." In this state "time, emotions, and thoughts seem surreal."[4]

In *memories of birth,* famous astronomer Dr. Carl Sagan postulates that the near-death experience might be a replay of birth where the baby passes through the birth channel into a bright, lighted room—with the doctor (often dressed in white) as a being of light!

Other things, such as illness and fever, can cause hallucinations. Brain tumors can sometimes cause visions of beings or sounds of conversations. Comas, seizures, brain injury, and even migraine headaches have all been associated with people seeing visions.[5]

But Gary Habermas and J. P. Moreland, writing in *Immortality: The Other Side of Death,* aren't so sure if any or all of the alternate explanations for NDEs can explain them away. They document cases where people who have "died" have told accurate stories about what was going on around them at the time of death—even private conversations going on in rooms near their hospital room. One young girl who came close to drowning in a pool was rescued and was hooked up to a lung machine for three days when her brain swelled up. When she totally recovered, she discussed details of the doctors' frantic efforts to save her and she claimed she was in heaven where she met "Jesus and the heavenly Father."[6] Others claimed to have died and found themselves in hell, while some learned about the deaths of others through their NDEs after seeing them on the other side.

Perhaps, Habermas and Moreland relate, there may be a link between these experiences and the next world through neurology. Wilder Penfield, the famous neurosurgeon, was able to connect the brain physiology with near-death. He studied the phenomenon by electrically stimulating the Sylvain fissure in the right temporal lobe of the brain. This might be "the discovery of the 'trigger' of the soul."[7] Habermas and Moreland explain that when Penfield stimulated it

> the patient would say, "I'm leaving my body now." Several patients reported, "I'm half in and half out." They also described phenomena like the experiences in the near-death studies, such as music, life review, and seeing "God or deceased friends." [Melvin] Morse [a famous figure in near-death studies] thinks that the "seat" for near-death experiences has now been discovered. He says, "By locating the area for NDEs within the brain, we have anatomy to back up the psychological experience. *We know where the circuit board is.*"[8]

The authors also point out that not many psychologists believe hallucinations are responsible for these types of NDEs (85), and the previously mentioned medical explanations can't adequately address the riddle of NDEs (86). Considering the extensive involvement with the occult by many leaders in near-death studies, they *do* believe occult involvement and Satanic counterfeiting is responsible for some NDEs.

But this does not mean that all near-death experiences are occultic and unbiblical. . . . this conclusion does not follow because counterfeit experiences presuppose genuine ones. Just as you can't have fake money without real money, so you can't have fake NDEs without real ones. You can't counterfeit what doesn't exist.[9]

When Does Death Begin?

Clouding this discussion is another fundamental question: When is someone who claims to be dead *really dead?* There have been cases in which people have been brought back to life even after they stopped breathing, had no vital signs, and had a flat EEG reading. In one case "a woman regained consciousness and lifted the sheet off of her face as she was being taken to the morgue by an orderly."[10]

Tal Brooke notes that Indian yogis have learned to slow down their heartbeats and enter a type of suspended animation, similar to death. Therefore, some NDEs may be occultic trances:

> Apart from some new category of deep dreaming, Moody's clinically dead may be in a state that is far closer to a mediumistic trance or a yogic *samadhi* than real death. In the *Tibetan Book of the Dead*, a majority of the predeath reports on death came from yogis who had learned to enter a type of suspended animation.[11]

Greeters on the Other Side

Another troubling element of NDEs that I believe strongly suggests satanic counterfeiting on the other side is that worldwide, these types of experiences don't match concerning *who* people meet upon journeying to the other side. Moody wrote that the identification of the being of light varied according to the background of the NDEer. "So, although some people believed that the being was Jesus Christ, others claimed the being was another holy personage, an angel, or simply just a being of light."[12] The troubling thing about this centers around Jesus and who he claims to be. The Bible is a very dogmatic and exclusive book. Besides Jesus declaring to be the *only* way of salvation (John 14:6) and the "one mediator between God and men" (1 Tim. 2:5), the apostles understood his message clearly even at the risk of persecution and death. Peter taken before the authorities declared this about Jesus:

> Neither is there salvation in any other: for there is none other name under heaven given among men, whereby we must be saved.
>
> Acts 4:12 KJV

My point is that if Jesus is truly the only way—and I believe he is—no one will be traveling down a dark tunnel to meet up with Buddha, Mohammed, Lord Krishna, Joseph Smith, or "a great universal spirit" following death. The leaders of Buddhism, Islam, Mormonism, and the other world religions taught things contrary to God's Word. There are not gods that rule over certain parts of the world who are responsible for only the people who believe in them, for we *all* must face the judgment seat of Christ (2 Cor. 5:10).[13]

Habermas and Moreland bring out another good point: There is no way for researchers on this side to verify the appearance—or identity—of any religious figure, be it Buddha, Mohammed, Jesus, or anyone else following death, even should they meet Elvis or JFK shrouded in a bright light. "In fact," they write, "how would these near-death patients know the identity of the religious personages *even if* they did see them?"[14]

When Eadie's story first began to take the nation by storm, and reporters began calling me asking what I thought of this resurgence in NDEs, I told the Religious News Service this, which was subsequently published in a number of publications: "It is very possible that if anyone is meeting someone on the other side, it is the old Angel of Light, whom the Bible calls Lucifer." I stand behind that quote.

"In both the United States and India, afterlife apparitions are commonly reported, but the experiences show many differences," reports cardiologist Maurice Rawlings in his book, *To Hell and Back.* "The Americans, predominantly Christian, tend to see only the supernatural being and later may encounter family and friends who have died before. The people of India, predominantly Hindu, do not usually see family or people, but do see some of their many gods or religious figures."[15]

Citing various studies, Habermas and Moreland report that religious, cultural, and sociological factors seem to influence reported near-death experiences. One study indicated that

> no American claimed to have seen Shiva, Rama, or Krishna. Americans also reported [seeing in an NDE] more than five times as many deceased figures as religious ones (66 percent to 12 percent, respectively). But Hindus, conversely, see almost twice as many religious figures as deceased ones (48 percent to 28 percent, respectively). Moreover, social factors seem to be at work with regard to the sex of those who are observed. While Americans perceived 61 percent female figures, Indians claimed only 23 percent. Even the Indian women reported twice as many male figures as female ones, all of which makes it tempting to claim that this

is perhaps due to the apparently lower status of women in Indian culture.[16]

After Death Comes Judgment

In most NDEs involving those from other religious cultures and even some experiences involving atheists and other non-Christians there is another similarity. Many claim to have been to a beautiful paradise. There is no judgment or punishment for wrongs, although some experience a review of their life. But as Moody's work indicated, and as illustrated in Dannion Brinkley's *Saved by the Light,* the being of light seems more interested in how the person has learned some lessons, rather than on punishing him or her for sins.

Therefore, we could conclude, perhaps, that these people did not finally die. Hebrews 9:27 states, "Man is destined to die once, and after that to face judgment."

Heavenly Visions

Pastor John Hinkle says he was awakened by the voice of God at 2 A.M., March 11, 1993. "His voice came to me a thousand times stronger than my voice is coming to you right now," Hinkle told his flock at the Christ Church in Los Angeles at Sunday's worship service three days later. "I heard it outside as well as inside. But, what he said startled me. And here is what he said: *'On Thursday, June the ninth, I will rip the evil out of this world.'* Now, immediately, I thought wait a minute! Nobody knows of what hour the Son of Man is coming. And I thought, *Is Satan trying to trick me into something?"*

But it wasn't Satan, Hinkle later said. It was God. "And at that time something cataclysmic of glory and power of God is going to come upon this earth . . . Now I didn't say the world's destruction," Hinkle continued in his rambling message. "I'm not prophesying that. I'm prophesying a cleansing. I'm saying what the Lord said to me . . . the veil that is spread over all nations [referring to Isaiah 25:7] . . . means all of the darkness that you see going on today. It's deception. . . . The veil that is spread over all nations, that's the veil I believe with all my heart I saw ripped asunder. He will swallow up death forever. . . . He has chosen to set this world free of darkness. Praise God. . . . And the glory of the Lord shall be revealed and *all flesh shall see it together* for the mouth of the Lord has spoken. . . . When that Glory comes, and come it will, there isn't anyone who won't be on his knees and on his face before God" (emphasis added).

Later Hinkle, who described the coming event as the greatest thing the world will ever see since the resurrection of Christ, said, "*all people* will see it at once" (emphasis added). He even added that following that day the curse of Babel will be reversed; God will "change the language of all peoples to one language."

"And when I saw . . . the ninth of June was Thursday in 1994," he continued, speaking to his stunned audience, "I tell you the hair on the back of my neck stood right straight up, and the power of God just shook me."

"Now you take it for what it's worth," he concluded. ". . . I have asked the Lord, as I said beforehand, if there is one word that I speak that is not from the Spirit of the Living God, destroy me, before I say it . . . I meant it 'cause I've never heard anything like this. It's too big!"[1]

Paul Crouch of the Trinity Broadcasting Network believed Hinkle's prophecy. He broadcast it before his large international TBN audience a few weeks later during TBN's twice-annual "Praise-A-Thon." And in Crouch's August 1993 TBN monthly newsletter, Paul Crouch used the "prophecy" as an incentive for people to hurry and give money to TBN to get in on the final harvest.[2]

Obviously, the great cleansing didn't happen, and the world appears to be just as evil as ever. Yet Hinkle, Crouch, and others did not repent for promoting error in the name of the Lord. In a tack that was amazingly like the Jehovah's Witnesses cult, Hinkle claimed that the evil *was* ripped out of the world June ninth, but that it was a spiritual veil that was invisible to the naked eye, and he said an earthquake that occurred *the day before* in Bolivia was a sign that it occurred: "Yes, I heard from Jesus," Hinkle boldly declared, "and, yes, he ripped the evil out of this world June the ninth."[3] In the case of the Jehovah's Witnesses, they began maintaining Christ did return in 1914 "spiritually"—invisibly—following the failure of "every eye to see" his return as the Scriptures declare (Rev. 1:7; Matt. 24:30; 26:64; Zech. 12:10). The Jehovah's Witnesses have gone on to set other dates (all of which have failed) for the battle of Armageddon.

Such failures based on exclusive visions and alleged "words from the Lord" have come and gone since the foundation of the Christian church. And they have at least three things in common: They shake the faith of individual believers; they damage the credibility of the Christian church; and they damage the unity of the Christian church.

In A.D. 156 a man named Montanus arose and declared himself to be the "Spirit of Truth"—the incarnation of the Holy Spirit who was to reveal things to come. He founded a movement in Phrygia, in west-central Asia Minor (now Turkey), a location where the gospel had great success.[4]

The movement steamrolled into hyper-charismania and mysticism as people began to see Montanus as a powerful "prophet" who was soon joined by two female "prophetesses," Priscia and Maximilla.[5] They began receiving messages they thought were coming from the other side in the form of ecstatic experiences and visions, and they labeled these "the Third Testament." One of their visions was that the kingdom of God was coming soon and that the New Jerusalem would soon descend from heaven and land in central Turkey, where it would become home for all the saints. The visionaries quickly sent word out to all Christians, summoning them to Phrygia to wait for the second coming.[6]

The movement grew throughout Asia Minor, spread to Africa, Rome, and even Gaul [France], and some of the top leaders in the young Christian church were swept up in it, including Tertullian, its most famous western theologian.[7] The movement didn't fizzle out even after the new Jerusalem failed to appear and other Montanist prophecies turned out to be false. Its followers continued to believe in the imminent arrival of the New Jerusalem. As I wrote in *Soothsayers of the Second Advent* (Fleming H. Revell, 1989),

> The movement divided Christians into camps of those who believed in the soon appearance of the New Jerusalem and those who didn't—continuous strife resulted. Finally the organized church acted. In 431 the Council of Ephesus condemned belief in the millennium as a superstitious aberration. But this really didn't put an end to it, according to [author Norman] Cohn. Traces of the movement could even be seen nine centuries later, in the Crusades, as the advancing armies of Europeans claimed to have seen the heavenly Jerusalem in the sky about to descend.[8]

Was the early church correct to condemn belief in the millennium as superstition? No, because the Bible strongly teaches of a coming golden era when the lion will lie down with the lamb, an era in which men, under the rulership of the Jewish messiah, will "beat their swords into plowshares." But some leaders in the church were correct to see the Montanist movement as it was— a false, divisive movement, rife with error. The Montanists had gone beyond what was written. They placed experience and false visions over the truth of God's Word, and that should have been enough to stop the movement dead in its tracks. If Montanus really was a prophet, then everything he claimed to have received from God would have come true. But it didn't.

Similarly, if John Hinkle really did hear from God, the evil would have been ripped out of the world on June 9, 1994. God would have made everyone see the truth as Hinkle described it—and he certainly would have begun his work of changing all the earth's languages into one by now. But sadly Hinkle's "prophecy" shouldn't have gotten out of the gate, much less have been promoted internationally by the world's largest Christian network and by a number of other charismatics and Pentecostals, including the *700 Club*.[9] It was *unbiblical* because God's Word declares that he will *not* rip the evil out of the world prior to Christ's second coming; and even during the millennium there will still be sin left on planet earth.

Yet today, men like Hinkle and other alleged prophets go on with their supposed words from God, and when they've been proven to be wrong they say, "So what? New Testament prophecies don't have to be accurate all the time." Thus they speak falsely in the name of God. Sadder still, top charismatic and Pentecostal leaders often prop them up and their ministries keep surviving—often growing, which damages unity within the body of Christ. Why? Because evangelicals and Christian fundamentalists who hold God's Word on a higher standard react with shame and sometimes horror at prognostications such as Hinkle's. They pull away from working with charismatics and Pentecostals and experience-driven Christians because of what they perceive as a lack of spiritual and scriptural discernment. The Bible tells us to "Test everything. Hold on to the good" (1 Thess. 5:21). First John 4:1 tells us to "not believe every spirit, but test the spirits to see whether they are from God, because many false prophets have gone out into the world."

When Is a Prophet a Prophet?

Biblically, when prophets told of the future they were always without error, and they were always specific—such as Christ being born in Bethlehem (Micah 5:2) and that he would ride into Jerusalem on a donkey (Zech. 9:9)—according to Dr. Ron Rhodes, an outstanding apologist and author. "To be a prophet in the sense of Jeremiah or Ezekiel means to be a direct mouthpiece for God," Rhodes notes, "and I don't see any justification for that" today.[10]

It is simply not true that prophetic utterances can be occasionally wrong in the New Testament era. The Bible's criteria for prophecy is clear. According to Deuteronomy 18:21–22, we are to judge prophets on the basis of their accuracy. "In Old Testament times, prophetic utterances that were any less than 100 percent correct were punished by death by stoning (Deut. 13:1–11)."[11]

In addition, I believe the Bible teaches that the Christian's maturity level, the soundness of his or her ministry and character over the long haul, coupled with fidelity to God's Word through sound doctrine, should also be part of the test we apply to Christian leaders—

especially if they claim unverifiable experiences or visions.

If tests like these were applied to believers throughout the centuries in situations such as bizarre claims about the New Jerusalem promoted by the Montanists, and subsequent strange visions of the heavenly realms recorded in church history, true believers would not have been swept away. When in doubt we should *not* believe strange revelations—especially some of the outlandish claims being put forward by some highly visible Christians today.

Jan Crouch

Jan Crouch of the Trinity Broadcasting Network has repeatedly told the story of how, through the power of the Holy Ghost, she was able to raise a chicken from the dead when she was a young girl. This story is absolutely untestable and about as verifiable as the children's stories in Medjugorje (of former Yugoslavia) who claimed to have seen apparitions of the virgin Mary. In another incident Crouch told her television audience that while riding in an airplane she looked out the portal and saw an angel flying on the wing wearing basketball sneakers! It's no secret to discerning Christians that the Crouches have not proven trustworthy in promoting sound doctrine and fidelity to the Scriptures in recent years on TBN. Among other things they have a fuzzy view of Christ's divinity, and they have actively promoted the lie that Christians can become "little gods."[12]

Kenneth E. Hagin

Much of the same can be said for the alleged supernatural visions of evangelists Benny Hinn and Kenneth E. Hagin. While Hinn's inconsistencies centering around his lavish lifestyle and questionable claims of faith healing have been exposed under the glare of the national media spotlight, many outside the Word-Faith camp in the church don't know much about Hagin. But he is one of today's more prominent visionaries who have claimed to have been to heaven and hell. And Hagin, who is sometimes called the founder of the faith movement, is influential. He is founder of the RHEMA Bible Training Center in Tulsa, Oklahoma, and his radio program, "Faith Seminar of the Air," is heard coast-to-coast and reaches more than eighty nations.

We should not necessarily believe any of Hagin's revelations. Why? By his own admission he was "excommunicated" by the Southern Baptists in 1937,[13] and he has proven to be a false teacher in important areas that undermine the uniqueness of Christ, even elevating man to his image. Hagin, in *Zoe: The God-Kind of Life,* asserts:

> Man . . . was created on terms of equality with God, and he could stand in God's presence without any consciousness of inferiority. . . . God has made us as much like Himself as possible. . . . He made us the same class of being that He is Himself. . . . Man lived in the realm of God. He lived on terms equal with God. . . . *[T]he believer is called Christ. . . . That's who we are; we're Christ!* [14]

In addition, there's little positive that can be said for Hagin's faith movement. A panel of cult experts at Evangelical Ministries to New Religions' national conference in Philadelphia on September 24, 1994, branded the Word-Faith movement as espoused by Hagin and others as "cultic" by a firm majority.[15]

Again, if someone—anyone—actively teaches doctrines contrary to God's Word, then how can we trust that their visions are from God? I make this point because Hagin has claimed trips to heaven and hell and a number of other bizarre experiences that are capable of stretching the credibility of even the most mystically minded.[16]

Radio Preacher Brother R. G. Stair

Internationally known radio preacher Brother R. G. Stair of Waltersboro, S.C., claims to be a prophet. God often uses him as a direct oracle to speak through, he claims. In early 1988 he heard directly from God, and Stair, who calls himself "God's end-time prophet to America," proceeded to dispense his prophecy to the rest of the world. With his voice thundering over the airwaves, he declared, using terminology of "thus saith the Lord," that before April 1988 was over, the United States would be thrown into economic collapse that would be worse than the Great Depression, followed by the forcible removal of President Ronald Reagan from office. Then before the end of 1988, a limited nuclear war would strike the United States, wiping out every major city. On national television, Stair even listed the cities to be hit[17] and he told a Philadelphia television show that if he was wrong he'd repent and get out of ministry.[18]

Obviously none of it ever happened, and after this writer documented in print that Stair's predictions, supposedly from God, were right zero out of seven times that year,[19] not only did Stair *not* step down, he began declaring that New Testament prophets don't have to be accurate. It also turned out in the course of this and other investigations that Stair was not above reproach both doctrinally and morally: Various people left his church (that they called a cult) disgruntled over Stair's lifestyle and doctrines. Yet today—six years later, in

1995—many Christian radio stations are accepting Stair's money in order for him to continue on the air calling himself "God's last-day prophet," giving new declarations about doomsday.

The Test of a True Prophet

In contrast, if something really does come from God it *has to come true,* and it is usually verifiable. Paul's vision of Christ on the Damascus road, for example, was verifiable. Not only was he *physically blinded* by the experience, but it was confirmed in Damascus by a second vision given to Ananias who didn't know Paul personally and was unaware at the time that Paul had been blinded. God further confirmed this by using Ananias in a healing role to solidify the two visions—thus verifying God's calling on Paul. God specifically told a fearful Ananias, who had known of Paul's (then Saul's) reputation as a persecutor of Christians, that Paul was his "chosen instrument to carry my name before the Gentiles" (Acts 9:15). Furthermore, during Paul's vision, the others traveling with Paul in his mission to persecute the church were aware of at least part of it. Acts 9:7 states they were left "speechless" by the experience. They heard the sound, but did not see anyone.

Verification can come in other ways. In Paul's vision or trip to the "third heaven," we find nothing that contradicts what the rest of God's Word had to say about that domain. And Paul did not impart any new insights about heaven. He said it was inexpressible and unlawful for him to talk about. And in John's vision of heaven, obviously we find that his fantastic description was not only biblical at the time, it also matched what was seen in the supernatural experience recounted in Ezekiel 1. Other parts of Revelation coincide with Ezekiel as well.

Changing Stories with Changing Times

History reveals that alleged visions of and trips to heaven have *not* been verifiable. Some have been blatantly unbiblical, with most of them being colored by the prevailing religious thought of the day. In other words, what the heaven visionaries claimed to have experienced in the dark ages differed dramatically from the heaven-hoppers of later times. So much for the immutability of God and the biblical declaration that "Jesus Christ is the same yesterday, today and forever" (Heb. 13:8). Apparently heaven, God's dwelling place, isn't the same every generation.

Of course, in the pre-Christian era, people still speculated about the next life. In Virgil's *Aeneid* some of the dead compete in games, while others are involved in training on grass and in sand. Ancient writers such as Plato called the next realm the "Isles of the Blest," and it was located above the stars.[20] In Plato's *Republic,* Plato also seems to have referred to an out-of-body experience.[21]

According to religious historian Colleen McDannell and Bernhard Lang's book, *Heaven: A History,* Christian visionaries throughout the centuries followed three models in their portrayals of heaven: the compensatory paradise of Irenaeus, the ascetic afterlife of the early Augustine, and the ecclesiastical model.[22] Much of the following historical survey section is borrowed from their book, and all page numbers in parentheses (in the rest of this chapter) refer to that work.

Various imaginations of, visions of, and alleged trips to heaven by Christians throughout history seemed to be influenced by the prevailing thought of the era in which they lived.

Irenaeus

Some early church leaders who witnessed savage persecution such as Irenaeus, bishop of Lyons (A.D. 140–200), seemed to have associated heaven with returning again to this earth. "They expected that after martyrdom they would experience an improved earthly existence," write McDannell and Lang. "They wanted to enjoy *this* world, not some imaginary heavenly realm. This belief was shared by their theologian, Irenaeus" (50). Further, the authors report, early church leaders strictly separated their new earthly existence in the kingdom of the Messiah following their deaths from the kingdom of God the Father. In their new earthly kingdom they would raise families and carry on business as usual (53).

Augustine's City of God

Several hundred years later Augustine, through a mystical rapture he shared with his mother, claimed to have touched divinity itself, experiencing a taste of heaven. He recalled that it was

> the greatest possible delights of our bodily senses, radiant as they might be with the brightest of corporeal light, could not be compared with the joys of that [eternal] life (55, 56).

In Augustine's monumental *City of God* (413–427) he formulated a doctrine he later called the "beatific vision," because in heaven "we shall have eternal leisure to see that He is God." There will be no work to do at all in heaven, no activities, nothing. Just "to stand, to see, to love, to praise [God]" (59). Thomas Aquinas continued with this picture of heaven hundreds of years later. He wrote that there will be no more active life in heaven—only perfect contemplation of God (89).

Is Heaven Rural or Urban?

Later in the Middle Ages some thought heaven was rural, while others thought it was a large city fashioned similar to the feudal city-state system of Europe where there would be castles. In an Inquisition document, a writer described heaven as having rural "beautiful groves and singing birds" an ideal climate (72). But Gerardesca (1210–1269) of Pisa, a reclusive woman prone to visions, contradicted that by portraying heaven as a "city-state with vast park-like territory" (74). She said the heavenly Jerusalem would be bounded by seven castles built on mountains circling the cities, with fortresses nearby. In the New Jerusalem itself would live the Trinity, the Virgin Mary, the holiest of saints, and choirs of angels (74).

Union with Christ

Still other visionary experiences shot far wide of the biblical record in the Middle Ages, and that was the case with female German mystic Mechthild (1207–1282) who claimed she had visited heaven through visions on a number of occasions. She said that heaven is not just one place, but "a series of distinct locations each with its own characteristics." In fact, she wrote, the lowest part of heaven is located in an inaccessible place somewhere on earth—and that's where she met Enoch and Elijah during one of her travels (100). McDannell and Lang tell more about her visions:

> In one of her visions Mechthild viewed the reception of souls into heaven from purgatory. All the newcom-

ers were given crowns, some of them by God himself. Thus God literally fulfilled the biblical promise, "Be faithful unto death, and I will give you the crown of life." The blessed sang and danced in adoration of the Trinity, and their song was answered with a flood of light issuing from the deity (100, 101).

However, Mechthild's alleged visions went much further, bordering on blasphemy. She claimed that in the highest heaven—an upper level—God resides, along with Christ's bridal chamber where he has sex with the holiest virgin women from earth. "During one of Mechthild's visits to heaven, she too was admitted into the 'secret chamber,'" report the authors, vividly describing her alleged physical encounter with Christ! (101).

Gertrude (1256–1302), who like Mechthild and other mystics, lived in the Cistercian convent of Helfta in Saxony, also had impure visions of Christ in heaven. She recorded them in her diary, the *Herald of Divine Love*. "In her visions Christ appeared to her in the form of 'a handsome youth of sixteen years, beautiful and amiable, attracting my heart and my outward eyes,'" she wrote (102). Elsewhere, the authors note, "Gertrude insisted on being a queen who shared both throne and bed with the heavenly king" (103). Gertrude, who later became a saint of the Roman Catholic Church, reportedly fell into numerous trances before her death, during which these sexual fantasies were confirmed, sometimes by "Jesus" himself.

Levels of Heaven

Several hundred years later, during the Renaissance, visionaries' pictures of heaven grew sharper with new details. In Dominican friar Savonarola's (1452–1498) book, *Compendium of Revelations,* he said heaven encir-

114

cled the universe and was above a high wall of precious stones. In heaven, he wrote, there were various levels connected by a huge ladder (118, 119). In the lowest levels were fields, flowers, live crystal streams, and "a large number of 'mild animals' (sheep, ermines, rabbits), all whiter than snow" (119). In higher levels were the thrones of Mary and the Trinity, and throughout heaven saints could float about without effort, not even needing the huge ladder connecting the levels (119).

Lorenzo Valla (1405–1457), a humanist theologian from Italy, also portrayed heaven as a domain where humans could float. He looked forward to going there to learn all the world's languages and to master all knowledge and to have a supernatural body. "We will play with our winged companions in the sky, upon mountains, in valleys, or at the seaside. Perhaps we will even be able to dive into the sea, spending time under water like fish" (128).

Into More Modern Times

Nineteenth-century Baptist preacher Charles Spurgeon (1834–1892) never claimed to have visited heaven. But he disliked the idea that heaven would be a place of contemplation and idleness. He preached from London's Metropolitan Tabernacle, perhaps reflecting the Victorian dislike for idleness, that heaven would be a "place of uninterrupted service. It is a land where they serve God day and night in his temple, and never know weariness, and never require to slumber," Spurgeon preached (279). Other preachers from that period on both sides of the Atlantic seemed to echo Spurgeon's sentiments.

But fanciful tales of the heavenly realm continued in the late nineteenth century, and they too, just as in our day, were written in popular books for the masses. Many were penned by spiritualists, and the public ate them up. *Strange Visitors* (1869) states that if people do not cultivate emotional sensitivity, heavenly hospitals and prisons would be waiting for them to serve in rehabilitating and healing sick souls. The book also describes a prison composed of transparent, polished seashells. In the 1898 book *Through the Mists,* heaven contains a "sanitarium for sectarians" where a fantastic otherworldly fountain helps invigorate souls. The author of the book also saw "heavenly amusement parks," strange special lounges, and plenty of sports such as tennis, rugby, soccer, cricket, boating, and dancing. People traveled via flying chariots, he reported (299–301). There were even authors who insisted upon seeing people's resurrected pets in heaven (300).

The Historical Response

Roman Catholic and Protestant theologians thoroughly rejected these accounts of heaven from nineteenth and early twentieth century spiritualists, fiction writers, and Protestant visionaries, report McDannell and Lang:

> "Such illusive drivel and profane trifling," wrote the Catholic bishop John Vaughan (1853–1925), "only disgusts and sickens one." The Presbyterian minister Robert Patterson assured his readers that the spiritualists were silly people who predicted that grandmother had knitting-needles in heaven and busily plied her "vocation in a land where there are no cold feet to need stockings!" (302).

McDannell and Lang correctly note that the nineteenth century church saw the spiritualists' views of heaven as a threat and used the opportunity to expose the differences between spiritualism and Christianity. Their heavens, either "ignored the existence of Christ or . . . presented him as 'the great social reformer' who teaches 'liberty without license'" (302).

Likewise, evangelicals should use visions of heaven promoted by the spiritualists of our day—Eadie, Brinkley, Steiger, Moody, and a host of others—to demonstrate the real Jesus of the Bible as opposed to their false ones.

Heaven-Hopping, Heresy, and the Occult

wen Shaw, founder of the End-Time Handmaidens, received an astounding prophecy from God in August 1990: the American armies gathering in Saudi Arabia for what was later to be known as Desert Storm were going to be slaughtered if America didn't repent and turn back to God.

"Yea, and I say unto thee that thou shall perish in the desert, if thou dost not reverse thy ways and come back to Me, America," God allegedly said, speaking through Shaw at Beaver Lake, Arkansas, Sunday, August 26.

"Yea, I say unto thee that there is a terrible demonic attack, even against the soldiers that have gathered together. Yea, and unless thou dost pray, this thing shall be unleashed and thou shall know such bloodshed as thou hast never known . . . if thou dost not seek the face of thy God with all earnestness and all humility—with all abasement, I say unto thee that thou shall sing, America . . . the greatest funeral dirge that thou hast ever sung!"[1]

Shaw was so certain her prophecy was from God that she published it, and noted that it "is meant for the entire body of Christ." The record, however, proves Gwen Shaw to be a false prophetess. America did not repent—and it is still sliding away from God. Yet months later in January and February 1991 it was the Iraqis who suffered horrible casualties as the U.S. and its allies ejected their once-proud army out of Kuwait. Iraq's losses were in the tens of thousands, while the U.S. lost less than one hundred—a number far less than the most optimistic estimates.

This failure has not stopped Shaw and other members of the Arkansas-based organization from continuing to prophesy. Each newsletter contains new words from the Lord, along with stories of encounters with the unseen world. Stories from the Handmaidens include visits with angels, trips to heaven and hell, bizarre meetings with the devil (sometimes casting out various types of demons), and strange tales about believers' identities as spiritual members of one of twelve tribes of Israel.

As previously mentioned in chapter 2, the End-Time Handmaidens, an organization that has followers worldwide, is a group fascinated by stories about trips to heaven and hell. Besides publishing several books about visionaries' trips to the other side, their catalog lists at least ten other books by authors who claim they've made mystical heaven- and/or hell-hopping trips (including some books by authors mentioned in this book). In addition, the Handmaidens' meetings and conventions often feature speakers who give riveting first-person accounts of trips to the other side.

Can We Trust in Christian Mysticism?

Perhaps a secondary theme of this book is that we should put all things to the test—especially subjective, mystical experiences. Because of a preponderance of false visions, revelations, and "words" from the Lord, it seems that discerning Christians cannot trust the mystical side of the church—even when their adherents seem well-meaning and claim that they are hearing directly from God.

Let's make one thing clear: There is nothing wrong with the charismatic and Pentecostal movements per se. The gifts of the Holy Spirit are for today. I believe all the gifts of the Holy Spirit are active today as Christ continues to build his church. God's Word tells us to despise not prophetic utterances (1 Thess. 5:20). The New Testament is filled with the supernatural events in the form of visions, signs and wonders, tongues,[2] angelic visitations, and even direct revelation via dreams.[3] Not all ecstatic or mystical experiences are false. In one case a relative claimed that following a heart attack, while awaiting heart surgery Jesus appeared in his room to assure him and told him he would have a complete recovery. No new doctrinal revelations were given, and the experience passed the test of time.

But all these things are to be subject to the Scriptures, and we are constantly told to watch out to make sure our doctrine is pure. In fact, if our doctrine is not pure—if we don't have a clear understanding of the gospel and the essentials of the Christian faith—our teachings on *any* aspect of God's revelation may also not be pure, and we are not qualified to be teaching anything from God's Word.

Those desiring to fulfill Christ's mandate to "make disciples of all the nations" must first meet the New Testament requirement of sound doctrine. Paul, giving his charge to Titus, tells him to "speak the things which are proper for sound doctrine" (Titus 2:1 NKJV). Later he tells Titus that his life should reflect "a pattern of good works; *in doctrine showing integrity*" (2:7 NKJV, emphasis mine). Paul tells his young convert Timothy to follow his *"doctrine,* manner of life, purpose, faith, longsuffering, love, perseverance" (2 Tim. 3:10 NKJV, emphasis mine). He adds that "All Scripture is given by inspiration of God, and is profitable for *doctrine,* for reproof, for correction in righteousness" (2 Tim. 3:16 NKJV, emphasis mine). Indeed, the term doctrine is used in the New Testament thirty-three times, with the vast majority of those usages having something to do with the fact that the church should uphold sound doctrine. Ephesians 4:14 states that "we should no longer be children, tossed to and fro and carried about with every wind of doctrine, by the trickery of men, in the cunning craftiness by which they lie in wait to deceive" (NKJV).

Is Mysticism Connected to Impure Doctrine?

The vast majority of those who weave fantastic stories about their trips to heaven and hell have at best made fuzzy statements that undermine essential Christian doctrine and at worst hold beliefs that are clearly unbiblical. There is a clear link between the rise of "heaven can't wait" and other mystical stories in the church today and bad doctrine. Many experience-driven Christians are not only easy prey to believe any new fad that comes into the church today, but they can also easily be caught up in the intrigue of these types of stories that can divert them from the simplicity of the gospel (2 Cor. 11:3).

More sinister is the possibility that many of these types of stories could have their origins in hell as a ruse to a sleeping church not willing to put all things to the test. If Christians' attention can be diverted away from the Great Commission and onto self, being titillated by stories of the hereafter, they become little earthly good for Christ's sake.

The Doctrine of the End-Time Handmaidens

This could be the case with the End-Time Handmaidens. In recent years several evangelical cult-watching organizations have issued warnings about the Handmaidens' doctrines, as various members have left that group claiming it is a "cult."[4]

The St. Louis-based national ministry Personal Freedom Outreach released a report quoting an ex-member who stated:

> The largest percentage of people involved in this cult are women who are either divorced, married to unsaved husbands, are in rebellion to their Christian husbands, "church-hoppers," unsubmissive to spiritual authority, are domineering toward their husbands, or are bitter toward men.[5]

It notes that founder Gwen Shaw, the former Gwen Bergman of Canada, founded the sect after "more than twenty-five years of wedlock and nearly a decade of separation" from her first husband, missionary Dave Schmidt, to whom she bore three sons and served with as a missionary to China, Taiwan, and Hong Kong. In the early 1970s she met retired Air Force officer, Lt. Col. James Shaw, to whom she announced that "the Lord has told me that I can marry you."[6]

The majority of the report hones in on the sect's false doctrine. Kurt Goedelman and Richard Fisher write:

The "Doctrinal Statement" of the Handmaidens, by orthodox standards, is vague and obscure. At best it has only one essential of Christian belief, the nature of God and even that is not clear. There is no distinct presentation of the Trinity.[7]

They go on to write that additional writings of Shaw contain other problems including the assertion that Christ "originally . . . shared the glory of the Father in heaven, and now He could only return to it through the gateway of suffering." To that the authors correctly respond that "Jesus did not suffer to earn back an inheritance. He suffered for mankind, so that people could have an inheritance."[8]

Other aberrant doctrines of the Handmaidens include the belief that Christians can be demon possessed. They also accept a major error of the positive confession or Word-Faith movement taught by Kenneth Hagin—that Christians can claim their healing and confess away any sickness or disease. Notes former Christian Research Institute researcher Bob Lyle:

[The] End-Time Handmaidens makes the mistake of including physical healing as part of the atonement of Christ. Rather than seeing healing as a benefit of the atonement it is a part of the atonement and thereby assured upon request. This is carried over to the animal world as well as for mankind.[9]

False Doctrine Learned in Heaven

It is perhaps little wonder, then, some Word-Faith adherents learned false doctrine in heaven. As discussed in chapter 2, Roberts Liardon and Jesse Duplantis both used their heavenly journeys to teach false doctrine, and chapter 3 shows that several books the Handmaidens publish teach falsehood. Still others' trips to heaven have not only taught false doctrine, but they have upheld other teachers and their false doctrines.

One such example of this is "faith" teacher Norvel Hayes's glimpse of eternity that he recounted on international television, November 13, 1990. After being transported to heaven on a "white cloud," he told TBN founders Paul and Jan Crouch, he met Jesus who rebuked him for not cursing the cause of growths on his daughter's body. "Whatever Kenneth Hagin can do in Jesus' name, you can do," Christ allegedly told Hayes. Upon returning Hayes claimed he used Hagin's principles of cursing the sickness and never doubting, and he was able to instantly eradicate the growths, although it took him forty days and nights.[10]

As we previously discussed, Hagin, the so-called father of the faith movement, not only teaches false doctrine that undermines some of the essentials of Christianity, but he claims to have traveled to heaven (and also to hell) where, he says, Jesus gave him a special anointing.

A Link to Holy Laughter

Perhaps it is no coincidence that Gwen Shaw's sect is now being linked to Rodney Howard-Browne and what has come to be known as the laughing revival.[11] Howard-Browne in turn has been credited with bringing the laughing revival to the Vineyard Christian Fellowship, an international movement that has been linked for a long time to strange experiences, including alleged trips to heaven and other realms. According to the Vineyard's literature, the laughing revival was injected in their movement after Randy Clark, pastor of the Vineyard Christian Fellowship of St. Louis, visited a Rodney Howard-Browne meeting and was overcome with a fresh anointing from the Holy Spirit. On January 20, 1994, Clark traveled to the Toronto Airport Vineyard, pastored by John Arnott, where he was invited to speak for four days. Allegedly, during the meetings, the fire of the Spirit fell on the church, bringing "revival" that's been accompanied with strange signs and wonders. It has resulted in more than a year of nightly meetings at the church as thousands of people have flown in from throughout the world to "receive the blessing."

The controversial Vineyard movement is under fire for allowing charismatic excesses to degenerate into outright occultism as many of its churches have seen bizarre, unbiblical incidents occurring during services under the guise of the laughing revival, or as they call it, "the Toronto blessing." Reports of Vineyard meetings being disrupted by people making animal noises, such as barking like dogs and roaring like lions all in the name of "Spirit-filled worship," are being spread throughout the U.S.[12]

I mention the word "experience" because that is the glue that tends to bring together many of the mystical happenings we've examined. Gwen Shaw reported that after she got hooked up with the Toronto Airport Vineyard and experienced "the blessing," her group also began having strange manifestations that she claims come from the Holy Spirit:

> As I heard the different testimonies and witnessed the way some of the men were literally "roaring" like lions, I wondered about that also. . . . I found that I, myself, had received the revelation of the roaring lion, but had forgotten it! [One pastor] told the hilarious story of the moving of the Spirit in his church. One guy was blowing the trumpet for hours—only he had no trumpet. He was doing it with his hands and his mouth.[13]

Although the phenomenon of holy laughter has its origins before the days of Rodney Howard-Browne, few would argue that his meetings represent the beginning point of the current "laughing revival." But what has not been reported extensively in the Christian press has been Howard-Browne's deviant doctrines presented in his talks and printed literature.

Rodney Howard-Browne is a mystic. He wants to see signs and wonders, he wants to see the mystical manifestations of the Holy Spirit. And he'll take experience over anything.

"I'd rather be in a church where the devil and the flesh are manifesting than in a church where nothing is happening because people are too afraid to manifest anything," he writes in his book *The Coming Revival*. "Every time there is a move of God, a few people will get excited, go overboard, and get in the flesh. Other believers will get upset, saying that couldn't be of God. Don't worry about it, either. Rejoice, because at least something is happening."[14]

According to the Personal Freedom Outreach, Howard-Browne, originally from South Africa, has other serious doctrinal deviations. First, he teaches Word-Faith doctrines such as guaranteed healing and the prosperity doctrine. Second, in promoting practices similar to astral projection and clairvoyance, he teaches some doctrines that are more at home with New Age occultism than with Christianity.[15]

But most serious is an apparent flawed view of the person of Christ and a confusion of the doctrine of the Trinity. Cult expert Richard Fisher explains that in contrast to the orthodox Christian view that Jesus on earth was fully God and fully human, Howard-Browne sees Jesus as "an earthly prophet who left His Deity in Heaven."[16] Howard-Browne writes in his book *The*

Touch of God: "Nothing Jesus did was because He was the Son of God. The Bible says He laid aside His royal robes of Deity and when He walked on earth He did so as a Prophet under the Abrahamic Covenant."[17]

To this Fisher retorts:

> Where does the Bible say that Jesus "laid aside His royal robes of Deity"? This is outlandish. There are numerous cults that see Jesus as only a prophet. It is unfortunate that this is taught by a "Christian" ministry. There are no verses produced by Howard-Browne even though he says, "the Bible says."[18]

Fisher goes on to write that Howard-Browne, as is the case of other Word-Faith teachers, has gleaned some of his theology from metaphysician and occultist E. W. Kenyon. In addition to Howard-Browne's practice of being a "Holy Ghost bartender" (during which people can laugh uncontrollably for hours on end), he claims the Holy Ghost can manifest himself at his meetings by forcing people to be "glued to the floor" where they sometimes have rapturous, mystical experiences—including out-of-body trips to heaven. But these experiences are only a small part of the physical manifestations to come, Howard-Browne says. "Very soon God will begin to miraculously transport people from place to place."[19]

Voices of Dissent

Almost as soon as various discernment ministries began looking into the views and manifestations surrounding Rodney Howard-Browne and the laughing revival, they threw up red warning flags. As of this writing not a single major or minor countercult ministry in the world has placed its stamp of approval on this alleged laughing "revival." Eastern Christian Outreach, Personal Freedom Outreach, the Spiritual Counterfeits Project, the Christian Research Institute, author Dave Hunt, and a host of other ministries are calling the movement a dangerous delusion. Most have gone even further and have labeled the Howard-Browne-spun movement as occultic.

The Spiritual Counterfeits Project, long-time experts in the occult and Eastern religion, was a bit more specific. It produced an article in its fall 1994 newsletter showing how the holy laughter phenomenon is also associated with non-Christian cults and Eastern antichrist gurus and their philosophies.[20] The implication, coupled with a scathing article denouncing holy laughter by former Eastern-mystic-turned-Christian Warren Smith, is that both the occultic forms of holy laughter, and the type advocated by Howard-Browne and others in the alleged revival, are coming from the same unholy source—the prince of darkness.

Yet, despite these warnings, some high-powered Christians such as Pat Robertson and the *700 Club,* Stephen Strang of *Charisma* magazine, and TBN's Paul and Jan Crouch, continue to endorse it and promote it, with few questions or scriptural tests.

Trips to Heaven from within the Vineyard

It seems that churches associated with the Vineyard Ministries International are ripe for any new "moves of the spirit" that come blowing through. Experiencing the power of God through "signs and wonders" has always been a hallmark of this movement that was founded by John Wimber. So it came as no surprise to many that Howard-Browne's strange new fire found

129

fertile soil in many of the estimated four hundred Vineyard churches nationwide.

Some Vineyard churches, however, who allowed members to roar like lions and make all sorts of strange animal noises in the name of the Holy Spirit have pushed it to extreme limits. When Wimber cut ties with a more established group of churches in the early 1980s—Chuck Smith's Calvary Chapel movement— there were warning signs that the group was heading in a wrong direction. One was a 1985 report about the Vineyard written by Robert Bowman and Elliot Miller of the Christian Research Institute that stated:

> There appears to be little emphasis on teaching the Bible per se. This lack stands in contrast to the very strong Bible teaching at Calvary Chapel, a church with which the Vineyard was once associated. . . . While Bible teaching is not emphasized enough, the role of experience in the Christian life appears to be somewhat over-emphasized. People in the Vineyard frequently seem to be willing to allow their spiritual experiences to be self-authenticating.[21]

Since that time this tendency has only gotten more pronounced. The Vineyard churches have faced scandals[22] and have delved deeply into the inner healing movement. In the late 1980s they absorbed the controversial, scandal-ridden Kansas City prophets movement, before they embraced the strange fire of holy laughter.

Most cult-watchers are beginning to echo the Christian Research Institute's loud alarm bells, charging that the Vineyards have arrived at an evil destination— occultism. Miller, one of the authors of the 1985 report, charged on his ministry's nationwide "Bible Answer Man" show that: "The dangers that we saw ten years ago [at the Vineyard] have gone even beyond our wildest expectations, then into full-blown occultism."[23]

CRI president Hank Hanegraaff went further on the same program, condemning the holy laughter phenomenon:

> This does not come from the Holy Spirit, this comes from the unholy spirit and it is dangerous and deadly. To the person who opens a doorway to the occult it is a very, very serious issue.[24]

The Kansas City Prophets

If Hanegraaff and other critics are correct, perhaps it was the Vineyard's flirting with the inner healing movement that led them to this point. Perhaps it was the Kansas City prophets it absorbed in the late 1980s that took them this far. Or more likely it was a combination of many things, along with Wimber's experience-oriented theology, that brought them to where they are today.

One thing is for sure: Each phase they went through prepared them to receive more supernatural experiences. First, inner healing teacher John Sandford (who has claimed a number of visionary and mystical experiences) began bringing his seminars to a number of Vineyard churches worldwide. You might remember Sandford from chapter 1 where he claimed he wrestled with a demon and a dead woman. Later it was a group of men known as the Kansas City prophets who brought grandiose claims that a "new breed" of super prophets were beginning to arrive on planet earth who would change the world forever.

These so-called prophets were a group of men that coalesced around a church known as the Kansas City

Fellowship, pastored by Mike Bickle, that attracted a following of other like-minded churches in that region. They argued that God was spearheading a new revival from their churches, and that he was restoring the office of prophet. Just as other "prophets" we discussed in these pages, yesterday's Kansas City stock could have it both ways. They could hear from God, and speak forth God's words, prophesying of great events soon to transpire on planet earth. And they could have flipped a coin as to whether what God allegedly told them would actually come true. *Often they didn't come true.*

Some of the main prophets and/or leaders in the movement included Paul Cain, Mike Bickle, Bob Jones, Rick Joyner, John Paul Jackson, Francis Frangipane, and others. Bob Jones (no relation to Bob Jones of Bob Jones University in South Carolina) was the visionary of the bunch. He was said to have been especially anointed with supernatural visions from the Lord and a prophetic gift. However, he was quoted as saying that the general level of prophetic revelation in the movement's "prophets" had an accuracy level of about 65 percent. Some prophets were as low as 10 percent accurate, he said, with some of the "most mature" prophets having a rating "approaching 85 percent to 95 percent."[25]

Similarly, the lack of accuracy in speaking for God didn't bother Wimber, either. Wimber soon became close to Cain and Bickle, and when the Kansas City Fellowship came under fire, Wimber saved them from even more criticism by absorbing the Kansas City Fellowship under the new name of the Metro Vineyard Fellowship. "Prophecy's first expressions will likely be infantile," wrote Wimber in the Vineyard's fall 1989 *Equipping the Saints* magazine that was devoted to embracing the prophetic movement. "Babies are messy and they make messes."[26]

Heaven: Kansas City Style

Aside from strange prophecies and visions, the Kansas City prophets reported visits to the supernatural realms, including heaven. In a series of five hour-long tapes entitled *Visions and Revelations,* Mike Bickle and Bob Jones are heard wowing followers of the Kansas City Fellowship with all sorts of tales of their unverified experiences in the next plane.

Bob Jones claims that when he was nine years old living in Arkansas, an angel carrying a "great trumpet" came riding down from the sky on a white horse and stopped before him in the middle of a dirt road. He didn't know what to make of it until he was thirteen, when he was escorted to the very throne room of God in heaven.

"You say that you saw the throne room?" Bickle asked him in the dialogue. ". . . what did it look like?"

"It looked like gold and it looked like light and it was a light not like the light you see here which is artificial," he responded, adding that the light, the glory of the Lord, frightened him. Well, a "guide," which he identified as "the angel of the Lord," protected him from danger by standing between him and the throne by filtering the rays from God as if the angel was "like red sunglasses."[27] He said he later understood that this was God's way of calling and commissioning him for their new important earth-changing work that could go out from America's Midwest.

Many years later, in August 1975, Bob Jones claims he had a near-death experience that was caused by a severe, painful nosebleed. He was whisked into heaven. Jones said:

> . . . all of a sudden, the pain was gone. And I was in a dark place and I looked around and I could see that I

was in a cave and I looked down there and then my thoughts were, "Oh, Lord, did I get my robe clean? Did I have enough time?" And there was a man that walked beside me and he said, "You can look now, Bob, and see" and I looked down and my robe was like crystal light.[28]

He then saw Jesus in the form of a light who would "grab and kiss" men and women of different ages—and then make them disappear by absorbing them into his body! "It was like two big ole doors right here in his heart and it'd be just that, and they was gone," Jones said. "They was in his heart." He then saw people that Jesus didn't want who were on "an elevator and an escalator" to hell which was like "a cold storage place." Jesus then commissioned him to touch the leaders in a new last days church so that he could absorb "a billion souls unto myself in the last day," Jones said.[29]

A short time later God "came and took me out of the body," and he descended into hell. It was "one of the most dreary, dreadful places I've ever been," Jones said. "It was like a place like a void, it had no top, bottom or nothing you could see—it was like black auto smoke and we went deeper and deeper into the depths."[30]

Mike Bickle's Visions

In the same tape series, Bickle and Jones relate the story of an angel revealing that God would appear to Bickle in the form of another person named "Don" in a vision or in a dream. Bickle said the vision eventually took place, and part of its message was to show him that "Jesus appears in thousands of different faces to portray something," Bickle said. "He was trying to say, 'I'm your friend, I am your familiar friend and I'm going to show you all things so you can move in the power of the Spirit.'"[31]

Later Bickle relates that during his trip to heaven Jesus commissioned him to be one of God's new generals to lead his end time army. Although Bickle claims he met with "the Lord" face-to-face, it was an out-of-body experience. It was 2:16 A.M. he said, and in a flash he was there, but it wasn't the cave where Jones earlier related he had been. Instead he was standing in a 20- by 30-foot room that "had clouds on the bottom, on the top and the walls." It was the courtroom of God. God was in the room, Bickle said, but rather than appearing as a being of light, he was a presence that Bickle wouldn't look at.

God rebuked him for not being patient enough in choosing leaders for his movement. Later the being ordered Bickle to ride in a golden chariot—one of about thirty-five—in a procession of leaders, apostles, and prophets, who would be joining the movement that would someday be worldwide. Bickle said that during the trip God did not commission him as an apostle. But he said he understood the experience to mean that if he was faithful he would "have an opportunity in the grace of God to fill an apostolic calling."[32]

What Are We to Make of These Visions?

Fortunately, the Kansas City prophets movement did not pass the test of time. Far from remaining a center-piece of Wimber's movement as was trumpeted in Vineyard publications not so long ago, this "new breed" of men that was going to help lead them have, by and large, fallen out of favor. Cain, who is no longer integrally associated with the Vineyards, has been soundly criticized for some of his pronouncements; even *Charisma* magazine associate editor J. Lee Grady pointed out a few of his false prophecies in his book, *What Happened to the Fire?*[33] More recently Cain unleashed a storm of controversy from within the Christian community when he released a supposed word from the Lord that President Bill Clinton, who has fought hard to keep abortion legal and whose first week in office saw him lobby hard to allow homosexuals to serve in the U.S. military, was God's man for the hour. He claimed God was going to give Clinton the power of the Holy Spirit to lead America away from a New World order.

Testing Doctrines

The fact of the matter is that Cain and other so-called Kansas City prophets should have never been placed into an area of Christian leadership in the first place. Cain (who has also claimed trips to heaven) has a questionable testimony, has demonstrated a lengthy absence of Christian service in his life, and he has called the late William Branham, with whom he once had an association, "the greatest prophet who ever lived." Branham, however, denied the historic doctrine of the Trinity (even claiming it comes from the devil), and taught extensive error, including the lie that the zodiac and Egyptian pyramids are on par with the authority of Scripture.[34] Branham taught what has now become known as the "Serpent Seed" doctrine that is popular with various neo-Nazi and "Christian" identity cults—that the Bible's Cain was produced through a sexual coupling between the serpent in the Garden of Eden and Eve.[35]

Bickle has been linked to the heretical Latter Rain and Manifest Sons of God doctrine that falsely elevates man into a god class. This also should disqualify him and his Kansas City movement from leading any Christian group in the future. In part 2 of Bickle's undated tape *The Glory and Dominion of Sonship,* he moves into blasphemy by declaring:

> My conviction is that one of the greatest transformations is when you begin to get the revelation that you are a Son of God. Son of God . . . God has conceived in His heart of a plan to make a race of men that would live like gods on the Earth. He has conceived in His heart to have Sons that would live like His Son, the Lord Jesus lived . . . That we were to be on earth the extension and manifestation of God's life in heaven.[36]

Although some voices have come forward objecting to critics' labeling some of the Kansas City prophets movement as promoting cultic doctrines, they don't have a case. Personal Freedom Outreach's Steve Cannon writes that "Bickle clearly uses unscriptural terminology and logic to teach Manifest Sons doctrine."[37] Despite this, Bickle is still popular in charismatic circles thanks to appearances on the Trinity Broadcasting Network and other charismatic media outlets.

Bob Jones, however, who not so long ago was regarded as the most powerful of the Kansas City crowd is out of ministry. First when Wimber's Vineyard absorbed the Kansas City Fellowship, Jones and another "prophet" were disciplined for making some outlandish statements and prophecies that were judged to have harmed some, and their prophecy tapes were removed from distribution. Jones's ministry was then limited to church leadership "behind closed doors."[38]

But it was behind those doors where Jones's ministry ended. Two women came forward in 1991 and told Vineyard leaders that Jones had used his prophetic authority to touch and fondle them sexually.[39] Jones admitted it and was removed from ministry. "In recent months, I have manipulated certain people for selfish reasons on the basis of my prophetic gifting," Jones said in a statement that he dictated and signed before the Metro Vineyard Fellowship senior leadership on November 4, 1991. "I have been guilty of sexual misconduct, and I deeply regret this. (I have not committed adultery.)"[40]

Many of Jones's and other Kansas City prophets' outlandish teachings and occultic-like practices and prophecies were documented in a dizzying 233-page report compiled by former charismatic pastor Ernie Gruen. Although Gruen later acknowledged that there were some minor inaccuracies in his report, it successfully exposed specifics of what he called the "charismatic heresy" of the Kansas City prophetic movement. Dates, times, and specific incidents of error (that sometimes caused great damage) and outright lies in the name of prophetic utterances were documented by Gruen's staff, implicating Bickle, Jones, and Jackson. I believe Gruen's work proved beyond the shadow of a doubt that the Kansas City prophets were false ones. We can therefore postulate that God has not spoken to any of these men.

God had some strict pronouncements against the false prophetic movement of Jeremiah's day: "Do not listen to what the prophets are prophesying to you; they fill you with false hopes," God spoke through the prophet. "They speak visions from their own minds, not from the mouth of the LORD" (23:16). A handful of verses later God calls them lying prophets, "who steal from one another words supposedly from me" (v. 30). They are leading people astray.

God's View
of Eternity

s the story goes, Protestant reformer Martin Luther heard that an interesting visitor was touring heaven with some new ideas. And so a heavenly meeting was set up between Luther (1483–1546) and famous Swedish mystic Emanuel Swedenborg (1688–1772). At the time of the meeting, which supposedly took place in the mid-eighteenth century, Luther had been dead for about two hundred years. It didn't matter though; Swedenborg was on one of his many out-of-body adventures to heaven that he would later go on to write sixteen books about.[1]

And it was during this meeting that Luther became convinced of the error of his ways, converted to Swedenborg's religion, and thus "he was slowly educated in heavenly matters. Only then could he move into a higher state of spiritual being."[2] Luther, you see, could not advance to a higher plane of heaven, and as a result was deposited in a lower part of heaven where he "received a house just like his earthly home" in Eiseben. "He did not achieve immediate bliss or eternal damnation for his arrogance and false beliefs," McDannell and Lang write, tongue in cheek. But Luther didn't convert without a fight. Swedenborg argued, with Luther "railing" against him, outraged that these new revelations had replaced his Protestant reforms.

Swedenborg convinced Luther, according to one authority, that he was able to release Luther's spirit in peace by causing Luther to repent of his "nefarious doctrine of justification by faith,"[3] which is the most profound and lasting truth of the Reformation!

Believe it or not, this is the story that Swedenborg passed off as really happening during one of his heavenly escapades. And Swedenborg for his day was not considered a nut. He was an intellectual who operated in the highest levels of academia and Swedish government, even reaching membership in the Swedish Diet.

The late Jan Karel Van Baalen writes:

> He was for thirty years the Royal Assessor of Mines, one of the body of men responsible to the government for the mineral wealth of Sweden. He wrote some thirty-three scientific works on metallurgy, mineralogy, physiology, geology, mathematics, cosmology, and the structure and functions of the human brain. He anticipated the airplane and the submarine. His name would have gone down in history as one of mankind's greatest scientists, but at fifty-nine years of age he resigned from his government post, and began to spend another twenty-five years investigating the things of the spirit, and wrote another thirty works, no small pamphlets either, on "theology," being firmly

convinced that the Lord had called him to revive a dying Church.[4]

Swedenborg thus became a cult leader, and today, nearly 220 years after his death, his spiritualistic movement is dying a slow death while Luther's principles live on.[5] Van Baalen notes that Swedenborg rewrote the Scriptures to make them square with his pantheism and spiritism, and he rejected the historic Christian doctrine of the Trinity, falsely believing the Holy Spirit was not a person, but a force.[6]

Swedenborg rejected Christ's vicarious atonement on the cross for the sins of the world, calling it an "abomination." He was also deeply involved in the occult. Developing mediumistic abilities, he was involved in automatic writing and clairaudience, and his reported trips to heaven (and other locations) were done via astral travel.[7]

Was Swedenborg's Heaven a By-product of the Occult?

Perhaps it was by opening himself up to the occult that the old angel of light, Lucifer, used it as a vehicle to start a new, false religion based in part on his romps in heaven and other spiritual realms. It is no coincidence that many other modern day heaven-hoppers and promoters of near-death experience "truths" also have been linked to the occult.

Swedenborg's heavenly trips share a commonality with many of those today promoting meeting "the light": He claimed an absence of judgment by God in the next world, and that hell simply doesn't exist (unless a person wants to send himself into an abyss after death), although a purgatory of sorts did. It sounds a lot like Betty Eadie's message. Note McDannell and Lang:

> From his [Swedenborg's] perspective, the idea that God judged the soul fundamentally good and worthy of heaven or fundamentally bad and destined for hell (or in need of a few years of purging) underestimated the goodness of God and the capabilities of humankind. Men and women were free agents who could choose good or evil, even after death.[8]

But beyond these commonalities with popular stories we hear about today, Swedenborg's visions of heaven are in a league by themselves. Not only do they contradict numerous biblical passages on heaven and hell, but they contradict virtually every other account of the great hereafter put forward by anyone else. He is one of the first to widely disseminate the unbiblical notion that following death, humans evolve into angels.[9] His stories of heavenly society contain wild tales of sexual experiences, bizarre accounts of angels' sexual practices, their writing styles, and even of male angels' beards. Some angelic communities, he went on to say, are similar to primitive African culture where people are carefree and walk around naked![10] And like the Mormon Church, he talked about the possibility of eternal marriage in heaven—though not necessarily to one's earthly spouse.[11]

L. Ron Hubbard

Another cult leader to weave strange stories of his visits to other realms (including heaven) was the late Church of Scientology founder, L. Ron Hubbard, who was also deeply involved in some of the darkest things of the occult. My book *UFOs in the New Age* showed how Hubbard, then a science-fiction writer, became an ardent member of Aleister Crowley's Ordo Templi Orientis (OTO) group just after World War II, which some have linked to satanism and occult ritual. According to an *English Sunday Times* journalist who interviewed people close to Hubbard and the OTO, Hubbard practiced witchcraft and acted as high priest during several occult rituals that included acts of sexual perversion.[12]

Crowley, who called himself "666, the Beast," and boasted that he was the most wicked man on earth, was allegedly the "first modern occultist to demonstrate the existence of superior alien intelligences," according to Kenneth Grant, Crowley's successor as head of the OTO Grant also stated that Hubbard had subsequent contact with extraterrestrials.[13] It turns out that Hubbard, too, claims to have had out-of-body experiences and visited heaven twice, along with destinations such as Venus and the Van Allen Radiation Belt.[14] *Cornerstone* magazine notes that Hubbard was willing to be specific about what he saw in paradise:

Of course [these visits] happened in his other life many trillions of years ago. The man is serious about these claims and even gives an exact date to his first visit of heaven—43,891,832,611,177 years, 344 days, 10 hours, 20 minutes and 40 seconds from the moment of revelation (probably during an auditing session) at 1:02 to 2 P.M. daylight Greenwich time, May 9, 1963. His description of heaven is as follows: "The gates of the first series are well done, well built. An avenue of statues of saints leads up to them. The gate pillars are surmounted by marble angels. The entering grounds are very well kept, laid out like Busch Gardens in Pasadena, so often seen in movies.

"The second series . . . is shabby. The vegetation is gone. The pillars are scruffy. The saints have vanished.

So have the angels. A sign on one (the left as you enter) says, 'This is heaven.' The right one says, 'Hell.'"[15]

What's the Difference?

As farfetched as Swedenborg and Hubbard's stories are, it's possible that they both were pulling off elaborate hoaxes on the public. It's also possible that their tales of heaven were designed as spoofs, although many more cult-watchers speak of Swedenborg's sincerity over Hubbard's. Both profited handsomely from the mythology of their new religions—both based on subjective experience. For all we know Hubbard and Swedenborg could have been con men, and in Hubbard's case many close to Scientology say that's exactly what he was. He simply fashioned his own cult out of the myths he created in his science fiction novels, they say. As I wrote in *UFOs in the New Age*:

> Speaking before a writer's conference in New Jersey in 1949, Hubbard said, "Writing for a penny a word is ridiculous. If a man really wanted to make a million dollars, the best way would be to start his own religion." After the publication of his 1950 book *Dianetics: The Modern Science of Mental Health*, that's exactly what he did; he founded Scientology.[16]

Similarly, what's to stop today's purveyors and merchandisers of their own encounters with "the Light" from making the whole thing up? After all, there are many motives for doing just that for the unscrupulous. Near-death experiences and "I went to heaven" stories are some of the hottest and most fascinating of all ideas being served up to the spiritually-starved public today. Good stories sell, especially the types of stories people want to hear. And spiritually good stories about experiences sell, not only financially, but if done right they can sway naive enthusiasts who are seeking a shepherd to follow—even if he is going to lead them off a cliff.

And in the Christian realm I suspect that some Christian publishers have sacrificed their integrity by publishing sensational stories about heaven and other unverified experiences. Veteran Christian journalist Ed Plowman, a friend of mine, told *ChristianWeek* that he believes that has happened. "Like their secular counterparts, some Christian book publishers are not immune to the wiles of market forces," Plowman said. "If they have a sensational story that will attract attention and sell a lot of books, they are prone to take short cuts from things like verification."[17]

Does Experience Matter?

But just because we cannot verify our experiences doesn't mean we should ignore them, either. There has to be a balance. Pastor Chuck Smith of Calvary Chapel in Costa Mesa, California, founder of the Calvary Chapel movement, says that biblical authority is the real issue when dealing with these difficult matters. Smith ought to know. He parted company with the Vineyard movement over some of the very issues raised in this book.

It is of utmost importance that we allow the Bible to be the final authority for our faith and practice. Any time we begin to allow experiences to become the criteria of doctrine or belief, we have lost biblical authority, and the inevitable result is confusion. There are so many people today who witness remarkable and exciting experiences. The Mormons, for example, "bear witness" to the experience of the truth of the Book of Mormon. They encourage people to pray in order to experience whether or not the Book of Mormon is true. One person says he has experienced that it is true, and another says he has experienced that it is false. Which one am I to believe? Each swears he has had a true experience from God; yet one has to be wrong. Whenever you open the door for experience to become the foundation or criterion for doctrinal truth, you are opening a Pandora's box. The result is that the truth is lost in the conflicting experiences, and the inevitable consequence is total confusion. We know that God is not the Author of confusion.[18]

Later in the same book, *Charisma vs. Charismania,* Smith calls unrestrained experiences drifting through the charismatic church "noxious wildfire."[19]

John MacArthur would agree. An outspoken opponent of Christian mysticism for years, MacArthur now believes a large portion of the church is losing its will to discern what is of God and what is not. That has become obvious with the so-called laughing revival and with those claiming authority based on supernatural visions and out-of-body experiences. He notes:

Mysticism is the idea that spiritual reality is found by looking inward. Mysticism is perfectly suited for religious existentialism; indeed, it is its inevitable consequence. The mystic disdains rational understanding and seeks truth instead through the feelings, the imagination, personal visions, inner voices, private illumination, or other purely subjective means. Objective truth becomes practically superfluous.

Mystical experiences are therefore self-authenticating; that is, they are not subject to any form of objective verification. They are unique to the person who experiences them. Since they do not arise from or depend upon any rational process, they are invulnerable to any refutation by rational means.[20]

And therein lies one of the dangers. If a sleeping church begins to accept almost every new experience as having a basis in truth, then it can accept almost any new story—even if it is unscriptural. This book has already shown where that has taken place. But the Bible has to be our final arbiter for truth. It must always rule over experience. God's Word tells us that "The grass withereth, the flower fadeth: but the word of our God shall stand for ever" (Isa. 40:8 KJV).

We Shouldn't Ignore Heaven, Either

But on the other hand, just because a growing chorus of experience-driven Christians are behaving strangely these days, that doesn't mean we shouldn't dwell from time to time on the unseen world. We don't have to believe the new stories surfacing about talks with Jesus when he whisked them into the third heaven. In fact we should reject them out of hand. But we *should* believe and look forward to walking with Jesus ourselves in a heaven that is fantastically beyond our ability to describe, a realm that can't be compared to any of the fanciful scenes of the next world given to us by those for whom heaven can't wait.

In heaven, time will be no more, and there will be no more sorrow. "And God shall wipe away all tears from their eyes; and there shall be no more death, neither sorrow, nor crying, neither shall there be any more pain: for the former things are passed away" (Rev. 21:4 KJV), the apostle John wrote from the Isle of Patmos following his heavenly vision and glimpse of the future.

Paul, who was also taken up to heaven, said we should comfort each other with the idea of being together with the Lord forever: "For the Lord himself shall descend from heaven with a shout, with the voice of the archangel, and with the trump of God: and the dead in Christ shall rise first: Then we which are alive and remain shall be caught up together with them in the clouds, to meet the Lord in the air: and so shall we ever be with the Lord. Wherefore comfort one another with these words" (1 Thess. 4:16–18 KJV).

Paul longed to be in his new body, one that would not be faced with earthly limitations. In one of the most beautiful passages of Scripture he writes:

> Now we know that if the earthly tent we live in is destroyed, we have a building from God, an eternal house in heaven, not built by human hands. Meanwhile we groan, longing to be clothed with our heavenly dwelling, because when we are clothed, we will not be found naked. For while we are in this tent, we groan and are burdened, because we do not wish to be unclothed but to be clothed with our heavenly dwelling, so that what is mortal may be swallowed up by life. Now it is God who has made us for this very purpose and has given us the Spirit as a deposit, guaranteeing what is to come. Therefore we are always confident and know that as long as we are at home in the body we are away from the Lord.
>
> 2 Corinthians 5:1–6

It is especially comforting that Jesus, the author and finisher of our faith, promised to personally prepare a place for us, and that when asked where it was by Thomas the disciple, Jesus emphatically answered him by declaring, "I am the way and the truth and the life. No one comes to the Father except through me" (John 14:6).

But Jesus also talked about another realm—a place of burning and gnashing of teeth, "the smoke of their torment ascendeth up for ever" (Rev. 14:11 KJV) for all those who don't accept Jesus as Savior, the only doorway to heaven—the true light not only of this world, but the light of the next one as well.

New Jerusalem

Why is it that none of today's visionaries describe the future city of God—the New Jerusalem that many of them claim they saw—in the same incredible dimensions painted on the pages of God's Word? It will be about 1,500 miles long, 1,500 miles deep, and 1,500 miles high, studded with almost every kind of precious stone imaginable, the Bible declares in Revelation 21! Scholars believe it will either be cube or pyramid shaped, the size roughly the distance from New York to Miami, then westward to beyond the Mississippi River, and just as tall as it is wide! It will literally come down out of heaven to a new earth (vv. 1–2) at the end of time. There we will dwell with Christ forever. Such a picture found in God's Word is well beyond the imagery given to us by *any* of history's most dazzling heaven-hoppers. Similarly, John's picture of the heavenly throne room in Revelation 4 is so fantastic that it is almost beyond our ability to comprehend.

"I did not see a temple in the city," John writes, "because the Lord God Almighty and the Lamb are its temple. The city does not need the sun or the moon to shine on it, for the glory of God gives it light, and the Lamb is its lamp. . . . And they will reign for ever and ever" (Rev. 21:22–23, 22:5b).

Questions or comments concerning the subject matter of this book should be addressed to:

William M. Alnor
Eastern Christian Outreach
P.O. Box 11322
Philadelphia, PA 19137-0322

Please enclose a self-addressed, stamped envelope. Write if you would like to be on the mailing list to receive our ministry's *Christian Sentinel* newsletter.

Notes

Introduction

1. Betty Eadie feature, prod. Steve Brand, *20/20,* ABC, 13 May 1994.
2. Ibid.
3. Raymond Moody, *Life after Life* (New York: Bantam, 1988), 4.
4. I do not mean to imply that Moody's foray into the occult is a recent happening. As we shall see, even before writing *Life after Life* Moody had been involved in occultic practices.
5. "Interview with Rodney Howard-Browne," *Praise the Lord,* Trinity Broadcasting Network, 23 August 1994.
6. Tal Brooke, "Near-Death Experiences: An Escape Route from Reality," *SCP Journal* 18:4/19:1 (1994): 12.
7. Ibid., 14.

Chapter 1: *A Magical Mystery Tour*

1. Roberts Liardon, *I Saw Heaven* (Tulsa: Harrison House, 1991), 25, 32, 38.
2. Ibid., 38.
3. John Sandford, "A Word from John," *Elijah House News* (August 1991), 2.
4. John and Paula Sandford, *The Transformation of the Inner Man* (Tulsa: Victory, 1982), 4–5.
5. "Evangelist Speaks of Ordeal Since January," Associated Press dispatch, 19 February 1987.
6. "A False Image?" *Philadelphia Inquirer,* 1 December 1980, sec. 15C.

7. Peter Popoff, *7 Hours in Heaven!* (Upland, Calif.: People United for Christ, Inc., 1993), 2.
8. Liardon, *I Saw Heaven,* 47.
9. Ibid., 42–43.
10. Ibid., 43–44.
11. See 2 Corinthians 11:17–18. Paul states: "In this self-confident boasting I am not talking as the Lord would, but as a fool. Since many are boasting in the way the world does, I too will boast."
12. John MacArthur, *Our Sufficiency in Christ* (Dallas: Word, 1991), 180.
13. Cho discusses this experience in his book, *Leap of Faith.* From "Interview with Dr. Paul Cho," Mary S. Relfe, undated, League of Prayer, P.O. Box 4038, Montgomery, AL 36104.
14. Ibid.
15. Kenneth Hagin, *I Believe in Visions,* 2d ed. (Tulsa: Faith Library Publications, 1984), 5.
16. Ibid., 44.
17. Ibid., 44, 45.
18. Ibid., 53–54.
19. Cerullo has also been in the news during this same time period as the focus of complaints centering on alleged fundraising improprieties and highly publicized allegations (especially in Great Britain) that his faith healing claims are fraudulent. In one reported case a woman whom Cerullo claimed to be healed died shortly thereafter.
20. Morris Cerullo, *From Judaism to Christianity* (San Diego: World Evangelism, 1962), 64.
21. Ibid., 66.

22. Ibid., 66–67.

23. Ibid., 69.

24. Jesse Duplantis, *Close Encounters of the God Kind,* undated videotape, produced by Voice of the Covenant ministries.

25. In his videotape, *Close Encounters of the God Kind,* Duplantis claims that babies who were aborted or lost at an early age have the opportunity of coming back to earth. "I saw those little souls at the throne of God," he said. "They could fly and they would fly into the presence of Jehovah and they would say, 'Can we be a spirit?' . . . I know why God sends those babies."

26. W. E. Vine, "Mansions," *An Expository Dictionary of New Testament Words* (Old Tappan, N.J.: Revell, 1966), 39, 40.

Chapter 2: *Writers of the Lost Realms*

1. Betty Malz, *My Glimpse of Eternity* (Old Tappan, N.J.: Chosen, 1977), 84.

2. Lorna Dueck, "Dream turned fact launches best-selling author," *ChristianWeek* (11 June 1991), 8.

3. Betty Malz, *Angels Watching Over Me* (Old Tappan, N.J.: Chosen, 1987), 16.

4. Richard Eby, *Caught Up into Paradise* (Old Tappan, N.J.: Revell, undated), 203.

5. Ibid., 228–29.

6. Ibid., 229–30.

7. Ibid., 230.

8. Ibid.

9. Richard Eby, *Didn't You Read My Book?* (Shippensburg, Pa.: Treasure House, 1991), 91.

10. Ibid., 96–97. Later after his experience Eby relates that God gave him an assurance that he really was his child again who was not bound for judgment.

11. Ibid., 92–93.

12. Ibid., 93–95.

13. The description of the Antichrist's demise in the same lake of fire is found in Revelation 19:19–20.

14. Mary K. Baxter, *A Divine Revelation of Hell* (Washington, D.C.: National Press, undated), 17–20.

15. Ibid., 151.

16. Rebecca Ruter Springer, *Intra Muros* (Jasper, Ark.: Engeltal Press, n.d.), 138, 158–59, 163.

17. Colleen McDannell and Bernhard Lang, *Heaven: A History* (New York: Vantage, 1990), 270.

18. Elwood Scott, *Paradise: The Holy City and the Glory of the Throne* (Jasper, Ark.: Engeltal Press, 1984), 89.

19. Ibid., 89, 91.

20. Aline Baxley, *I Walked in Hell* (Jasper, Ark.: End-Time Handmaidens, undated), 3.

21. G. Richard Fisher, "Heaven Hopping," *Personal Freedom Outreach Newsletter* (October–December 1985): 4.

22. "Irene Wakabi of Uganda," Advocate International Ministries, n.d., 418 10th St., #28, Sacramento, CA 95814.

23. Ralph Wilkerson, *Beyond and Back* (Anaheim: Melodyland Productions, 1977), 92.

24. Gordon Lindsay, ed., *Scenes Beyond the Grave,* 36th ed. (Dallas: Christ for the Nations, n.d.), 9.

25. Ibid., 24.

26. Ibid., 62.

27. Robert Morey, *Death and the Afterlife* (Minneapolis: Bethany, 1984), 88.

28. Gary R. Habermas and J. P. Moreland, *Immortality: The Other Side of Death* (Nashville: Thomas Nelson, 1992), 93.

29. Brooks Alexander, "Angels in Scripture and Superstition," *SCP Journal* 18:4/19:1 (1994): 59.

Chapter 3: *Embraced by the Darkness*

1. Jim Jerome, "Heaven Can Wait," *People,* 81, quoted in Richard Abanes, *Embraced by the Light and the Bible* (Camp Hill, Pa.: Christian Publications, 1994), 203.

2. Betty Eadie, *American Journal,* February 1994, quoted in Abanes, *Embraced by the Light,* 203.

3. Craig Branch, "Clues to a Near-Death Experience: Betty Eadie's Other Source," *SCP Journal* 18:4/19:1 (1994): 40.

4. Abanes, *Embraced by the Light,* 208.

5. Branch, "Clues to a Near-Death Experience," 40.

6. Betty Eadie, *Embraced by the Light* (Placerville, Calif.: Gold Leaf Press, 1992), 98–99.

7. G. Richard Fisher with M. Kurt Goedelman, "Embraced By the Darkness:

Notes

Betty Eadie's Old Errors in New Age Dress," *The Quarterly Journal* 14, no. 2 (April–June 1994): 11.

8. Letters to the editor, *Charisma* (September 1994): 10.

9. Warren Smith, "Embracing a False Light," *SCP Journal* 18:4/19:1 (1994): 23.

10. Richard Abanes and Paul Carden, "A Special Report: What Is Betty Eadie Hiding?" *Christian Research Journal* (winter 1994): 40.

11. Abanes, *Embraced by the Light,* 215.

12. Branch, "Clues to a Near-Death Experience," 40.

13. Orthodox Christianity teaches that humankind is separate from God, separate in substance from other objects, and that God is separate from his creation.

14. Smith, "Embracing a False Light," 25.

15. Eadie, *Embraced by the Light,* 95.

16. Abanes, *Embraced by the Light,* 220.

17. Smith, "Embracing a False Light," 17.

18. Ibid., 21.

19. Ibid., 25.

20. Dannion Brinkley, *Saved by the Light* (New York: Villard, 1994), 72.

21. Ibid., 40.

22. Ibid., 46.

23. Brad Steiger, *One with the Light* (New York: Signet, 1994), 289.

24. Ibid., 292–297.

25. Ibid., 295.

26. Ibid., 300.

Chapter 4: *Near-Death Experiences, Spiritism, and the Occult*

1. See my book, *UFOs in the New Age: Extraterrestrial Messages and the Truth of Scripture* (Grand Rapids: Baker, 1992) for more details.

2. Jon Klimo, *Channeling* (Los Angeles: Jeremy Tarcher, 1987), 5–6.

3. Brad Steiger's 1983 book, *Gods of Aquarius,* lists seven ways of channeling: trance or sleep mediumship/channeling; automatic writing, drawing, or music; clairaudience (clear hearing), clairvoyance (clear seeing), clairsentience (clear sensing of feeling); mental telepathy or thought transference; space beams; inspiration, intuition, or hunches; and the "I-Am" consciousness.

4. Elijah, however, had never died. See 2 Kings 2.

5. Abanes, *Embraced by the Light,* 130.

6. Eadie, *Embraced by the Light,* 58, 79.

7. *Oprah Winfrey Show,* 2 January 1994, quoted in Abanes, *Embraced by the Light,* 137.

8. Lennie Kronisch, "Elisabeth Kübler-Ross: Messenger of Love," *Yoga Journal* (November/December 1976): 18, quoted in Mark Albrecht and Brooks Alexander, "Thanatology: Death and Dying," *SCP Journal* (April 1977): 7–8.

9. Albrecht and Alexander, "Thanatology," 8.

10. Abanes, *Embraced by the Light,* 152.

11. Albrecht and Alexander, "Thanatology," 6.

12. A version of the book *Lord of the Air: Tales of a Modern Antichrist* was released by Harvest House in 1990.

13. Albrecht and Alexander, "Thanatology," 7.

14. Tal Brooke, *The Other Side of Death: Does Death Seal Your Destiny?* (Wheaton: Tyndale House, 1979), 34.

15. Albrecht and Alexander, "Thanatology," 8.

16. Abanes, *Embraced by the Light,* 166.

17. This was further confirmed in an interview by the author with one of Ritchie's close relatives.

18. Brooke, *Other Side of Death,* 37.

19. Ibid.

20. Alnor, *UFOs in the New Age,* 114.

21. Brooke, *Other Side of Death,* 40.

22. Brooke, "Near-Death Experiences," 12.

Chapter 5: *What Is Death, Anyway?*

1. J. Isamu Yamamoto, "The Near-Death Experience," part 1: "The New Age Connection," *Christian Research Journal* (spring 1992): 21–32; part 2: "Alternative Explanations" (summer 1992): 14–29.

2. Susan Blackmore, *20/20,* ABC, 13 May 1994.

3. J. Isamu Yamamoto, "Near-Death Experience," part 2, 16.

4. Ibid.

5. Rusty Wright, *The Other Side of Life* (San Bernardino, Calif.: Here's Life, 1979), 17–25.

6. Habermas and Moreland, *Immortality,* 75–76.

7. Ibid., 83.

8. Ibid.

9. Ibid., 93.

10. Ibid., 77.

11. Tal Brooke, "Near-Death Experiences," 8.

12. J. Isamu Yamamoto, "Near-Death Experience," part 1, 30.

13. The Bible, however, seems to indicate in Romans 2 that people who have not heard about the law—and presumably God's way of salvation through Jesus Christ—may fall under a different standard of judgment that has something to do with the light that they have, namely their consciences. This in no way obstructs the biblical principle that Jesus is the only door through which men can be saved. See Romans 3:21–31.

14. Habermas and Moreland, *Immortality,* 90–91.

15. Maurice Rawlings, *To Hell and Back* (Nashville: Thomas Nelson, 1983), 10, 79.

16. Habermas and Moreland, *Immortality,* 90–91.

Chapter 6: *Heavenly Visions*

1. John Hinkle, "Thy Kingdom Come," message at Christ Church, Los Angeles, 3 March 1993.

2. Jackie Alnor, "The 'Cleansing': The Removal of the Wicked, set for 9 June 1994," *The Christian Sentinel* 2, nos. 1–2 (September 1993): 11. This article contains the transcript of much of Hinkle's prophecy. *The Christian Sentinel* is published by Eastern Christian Outreach, P.O. Box 11322, Philadelphia, PA 19137-0322.

3. Jackie Alnor, "Update on the 'Cleansing'—It Was Only a Shaking," *The Christian Sentinel* 3, nos. 1–2 (September 1994): 20.

4. William M. Alnor, *Soothsayers of the Second Advent* (Old Tappan, N.J.: Revell, 1989), 54. In fact, John's letters to the seven churches in the Book of Revelation were located in Phrygia.

5. William M. Alnor, "When Heaven Can't Wait," *SCP Journal* 18:4/19:1 (1994): 43.

6. Norman Cohn, *The Pursuit of the Millennium,* 2d ed. (New York: Harper Torchbooks, 1961), 21.

7. Ibid.

8. Cohn, *Pursuit of the Millennium,* 9, 14.

9. A Youth with a Mission official also confirmed the June 9 prophecy, and on the June 9 telecast of the *700 Club,* which is a production of Pat Robertson's Christian Broadcasting Network, Robertson and cohost Ben Kinchlow promoted the "prophecy" by stating that the Bolivian earthquake may have had something to do with its fulfillment.

10. William M. Alnor, "Are There Prophets Today?" *The Christian Sentinel* 3, nos. 1–2 (September 1994): 24.

11. Alnor, *Soothsayers of the Second Advent,* 40.

12. See Hank Hanegraaff, *Christianity in Crisis* (Eugene, Ore.: Harvest House, 1983) for more details. Of TBN Hanegraaff writes on pages 38 and 39, "What many of those who support TBN do not know, however, is that part of this money goes to promoting cultic groups and individuals who not only deny the Trinity but claim that this essential of Christianity is a pagan doctrine. It is indeed ironic that a broadcasting network called 'Trinity' would promote anti-trinitarian doctrine."

13. Ibid., 333.

14. Kenneth E. Hagin, *Zoe: The God-Kind of Life* (Tulsa: Kenneth Hagin Ministries, 1989), 35–36, 41.

15. This author, William M. Alnor, is executive director and vice president of Evangelical Ministries to New Religions (EMNR). For information on EMNR or to receive tapes from the Philadelphia conference write EMNR, P.O. Box 20352, Philadelphia, PA 19137-0352.

16. See Kenneth E. Hagin's book, *I Believe in Visions,* 2d ed. (Tulsa: Kenneth Hagin Ministries, 1989), and Hanegraaff, *Christianity in Crisis,* which recounts some of Hagin's visions.

17. "Church of Doom," *A Current Affair,* Fox Broadcasting, May 1988.

18. R. G. Stair, interview by Wally Kennedy, *AM Philadelphia,* May 1988.

19. William and Jacqueline Alnor, "Prophet Strikes Out," *Delaware County*

(Pa.) Daily Times, 14 February 1989, p. 32. In addition, the author has written many articles about Stair and his cult, most of them published in the *Delaware County Daily Times,* Primos, PA.

20. McDannell and Lang, *Heaven,* 16.
21. Wright, *Other Side of Life,* 3.
22. McDannell and Lang, *Heaven,* 48.

Chapter 7: *Heaven-Hopping, Heresy, and the Occult*

1. Gwen R. Shaw, "Prophecy for the Church and America. Re: Persian Gulf/Iraq-Kuwait Emergency," prophecy given at Zebulun Haven, Beaver Lake, Ark., 26 August 1990. Published by the End-Time Handmaidens.
2. This does not mean that all believers must speak in tongues, as is sometimes taught in Pentecostal/charismatic circles. Nowhere does the New Testament even imply that most Christians will experience the gift of tongues. Paul writes in 1 Corinthians 12:30: "Do all speak in tongues?"
3. See Acts 16:9.
4. My own ministry, Eastern Christian Outreach, has received chilling testimonies from people who have left that organization.
5. M. Kurt Goedelman with G. Richard Fisher, "End-Time Handmaidens: Ministry for the Last Days or 'End-Time' Delusion?" *The Quarterly Journal,* 14, no. 3 (1994): 5. To contact PFO write P.O. Box 26062, St. Louis, MO 63136.
6. Ibid.
7. Ibid.
8. Ibid.
9. Robert Lyle, Research Consultant, "End-Time Handmaidens," evaluation by the Christian Research Institute, March 1989, 2. To obtain a copy write CRI, P.O. Box 500, San Juan Capistrano, CA 92693.
10. Hanegraaff, *Christianity in Crisis,* 78–79.
11. The types of experiences taking place in this so-called "revival" in no way match revivals of previous centuries. The author believes the so-called "laughing revival" is a satanic counterfeit.
12. This writer personally visited the Valley Forge, Pa., Vineyard 5 November

1994 and was disturbed to see all types of strange behavior that included primal screams, people rolling around in aisles, uncontrollable laughing and shaking, the casting out of demons from Christians, bizarre words of knowledge, and people making animal noises. As a result, Eastern Christian Outreach produced a tract entitled "This is no laughing matter," warning against this type of behavior. Write P.O. Box 11322, Philadelphia, PA 19137-0322.

13. Gwen Shaw, "The 'Toronto Blessing' is Real!" *End-Time Handmaidens Magazine* (November 1995): 1, 18.
14. Rodney Howard-Browne, *The Coming Revival,* 6, 8, quoted in G. Richard Fisher, "A Look at Spiritual Pandemonium: The Strange Views of Rodney M. Howard-Browne," *The Quarterly Journal* 14, no. 4 (October–December 1994): 13.
15. Ibid., 14.
16. Ibid., 15, 16.
17. Rodney Howard-Browne, *The Touch of God,* 13–14, quoted in Fisher, "A Look at Spiritual Pandemonium," 16.
18. Fisher, "A Look at Spiritual Pandemonium," 16.
19. Rodney Howard-Browne, *The Reality of the Person of the Holy Spirit,* quoted in Fisher, "A Look at Spiritual Pandemonium," 14.
20. Warren Smith and Danny Aguirre, "Some Examples of Holy Laughter in Other Religions," *SCP Newsletter* (fall 1994): 14.
21. Elliot Miller and Robert Bowman Jr., *The Vineyard* (San Juan Capistrano, Calif.: Christian Research Institute, February 1985).
22. Writer Al Dager notes, "Wimber had to face the fact that scandals were plaguing the Vineyard leadership. Admissions of adultery, lying, drunkenness, revelry, and licentiousness of all types among the pastors of the Vineyard have raised questions as to whether or not God is in their midst." In citing Wimber's undated tape, *Unpacking Your Bags,* Dager wrote in a special report released around the time of the Kansas City Fellowship's incorporation into the Vineyard that "Wimber has stated that even he has felt far from God for several years." Cited in Dager's undated *Media*

Spotlight special report entitled "Latter Day Prophets," 20.

23. Elliot Miller, *The Bible Answer Man Show,* Christian Research Institute, 2 November 1994.

24. Hank Hanegraaff, *The Bible Answer Man Show,* Christian Research Institute, 2 November 1994.

25. Steven F. Cannon, "Old Wine in Old Wineskins: A Look at Kansas City Fellowship," *The Quarterly Journal* 10, no. 4 (October–December 1990): 8.

26. William M. Alnor and Robert Lyle, "Controversial Prophetic Movement is Incorporated into the Vineyard," *Christian Research Journal* (fall 1990): 5–6.

27. Mike Bickle with Bob Jones, *Visions and Revelations,* transcript, series of five tapes from the fall of 1988, 1–3.

28. Ibid., 14, 15.

29. Ibid., 15.

30. Ibid., 16.

31. Ibid., 53–60.

32. Ibid., 80–82.

33. J. Lee Grady, *What Happened to the Fire?* (Grand Rapids: Chosen, 1994), 114–17.

34. See my book *Soothsayers of the Second Advent* for further information on so-called Christian astrology and pyramidology.

35. Dager, "Latter Day Prophets," 2.

36. Cannon, "Old Wine in Old Wineskins," 10.

37. Ibid.

38. Alnor and Lyle, "Controversial Prophetic Movement," 5.

39. Roy Rivenburg, "A Question of Faith," *Los Angeles Times,* 28 January 1992, sec. E1, p. 8.

40. Copy of Jones's letter on file, as well as other documents related to the scandal.

Chapter 8: *God's View of Eternity*

1. McDannell and Lang, *Heaven,* 182.

2. Ibid., 188.

3. Jan Karel Van Baalen, *The Chaos of Cults* (Grand Rapids: Eerdmans, 1956), 345.

4. Ibid., 341, 324.

5. According to Bob Larson, *Larson's Book of Cults* (Wheaton: Tyndale House, 1982), 397, Swedenborg's U.S. followers number about 20,000 "and at least 100,000 others worldwide." Other cult experts place their numbers far lower.

6. Ibid., 342, 345.

7. Ibid., 78.

8. McDannell and Lang, *Heaven,* 200.

9. This contradicts Scripture. In Matthew 22:30 and Mark 12:25 Jesus tells us that we will be "like the angels" in heaven in the sense that we will not marry. But we will not be angels. Paul states in 1 Corinthians 6:3 that someday the saints will judge the angels.

10. McDannell and Lang, *Heaven,* 219.

11. Ibid., 218.

12. "Cult of the Month—Scientology: Pandora's Box," *Cornerstone* 31 (1976): 11, 16, 23.

13. Kenneth Grant, *Outside the Circles of Time* (London: Frederick Muller, 1980), 18 and jacket cover.

14. "Cult of the Month," 11, 16, 23.

15. Ibid.

16. Ibid.

17. Dueck, "Dream turned fact," 2.

18. Chuck Smith, *Charisma vs. Charismania* (Eugene, Ore.: Harvest House, 1983), 127.

19. Ibid., 151.

20. John MacArthur, *Reckless Faith: When the Church Loses Its Will to Discern* (Wheaton: Crossway, 1994), 27.

General Index

Abanes, Richard, 60, 64–66, 83
Aeneid (Virgil), 111
Albrecht, Mark, 80–81
Alexander, Brooks, 58, 80–81
Angels Watching Over Me (Malz), 46
Association for Research and Enlightenment (ARE), 85
Augustine, 112

Baxley, Aline, 54
Baxter, Mary K., 51–52
Beyond and Back (Wilkerson), 55–56
Bickle, Mike, 132–37
Blackmore, Susan, 94
Bowman, Robert, 130
Branch, Craig, 60
Branham, William, 136
Brinkley, Dannion, 23, 67–71
Brooke, Tal, 24–25, 82–83, 85, 97

Cain, Paul, 132, 135–36
Calvary Chapel movement, 130, 145
Cannon, Steve, 137
Caught Up into Paradise (Eby), 47–48
Cayce, Edgar, 85–86
Cerullo, Morris, 38
channeling, 75–79
Cho, David (Paul) Yonggi, 36
City of God (Augustine), 112
Collett, Percy, 54–55
counterfeit Christs, 43, 73–74, 86–87
Crouch, Jan, 107, 129
Crouch, Paul, 102, 129
Crowley, Aleister, 143

Davis, Marietta, 56

deception, 23, 43, 73–74, 86–87
demonic, visions of, 30–31
Demons: An Eyewitness Account (Pittman), 55
Dianetics: The Modern Science of Mental Health (Hubbard), 144
Didn't You Read My Book? (Eby), 48–50
Divine Comedy, The (Dante), 51
Divine Revelation of Hell, A (Baxter), 51–52
doctrine, testing of, 106, 121–25, 136–38
Dueck, Lorna, 46
Duplantis, Jesse, 39–40

Eadie, Betty, 17–18, 23, 59–67, 79–80, 94
Eby, Richard, 20, 47–50
Embraced by the Light (Eadie), 17–18, 23, 59–67
Embraced by the Light: Betty Eadie and Near-Death Experiences in the Light of Scripture (Abanes), 60, 64–65
End-Time Handmaidens, 52–57, 119–20, 123–24
end times, 72–74
Equipping the Saints magazine, 132

"familiar spirits," 76
in the New Testament, 78–79
Fisher, G. Richard, 62, 123–24, 127–28

Gerardesca of Pisa, 113
Gertrude, 114
Goedelman, M. Kurt, 62, 123–24
Gold Leaf Press, 64–65

Grady, J. Lee, 136
Grant, Kenneth, 143
Gruen, Ernie, 138

Habermas, Gary, 57–58, 95–100
Hagin, Kenneth E., 36–37, 107–9, 125
Hanegraaff, Hank, 131
Hayes, Norvel, 125
heaven
biblical view of, 39–41
Christian anticipation of, 39–40, 147–49
Paul's visit to, 34–35, 40–41
visits to, 31–39
Heaven: A History (McDannell and Lang), 111–16
heavenly mansions, 41–43
hell, 50–51, 57
Hinkle, John, 101–3, 105
Hinn, Benny, 28–29, 107–8
"holy laughter" movement, 21–22, 125–28, 130
Howard-Browne, Rodney, 21–22, 125–28
Hubbard, L. Ron, 142–44

I Believe in Visions (Hagin), 36–37
Intra Muros (Springer), 53
Irenaeus, 112
I Saw Heaven (Liardon), 27–28

Jehovah's Witnesses, 103
Jones, Bob (Kansas City Fellowship), 132–34, 137–38
Journal of Discourse, 68
Journeys Out of the Body (Monroe), 81–82
judgment, God's, 61–62, 77–79, 100, 148–49

General Index

Scripture Index